To Bernard Vick and my other teachers over the years, who taught me to think, and Father Alan Cox, a priest, who taught me to act, and to my loving family; Christine, Kelly and James, who have borne the consequences without complaint.

—*Barry Sheehy*

To my friends and business associates, Jack Rosenblum, Aubrey Sanford, and Roy Trueblood, who prepared me for this stage in my career; to the clients and employees of The Atlanta Consulting Group, who have been my teachers; and to my beautiful wife, Cass Flagg, for her loving support.

—*Hyler Bracey*

To my parents, Helen and Richard.

—*Rick Frazier*

TABLE OF CONTENTS

Acknowledgments

James O'Toole, Executive Director of The Leadership Institute and long-time moderator of the Aspen Institute Executive Seminar, has a rule which states, "Whenever about to congratulate oneself on having an original idea, before going public, remind yourself that the odds are, Aristotle had it first!" O'Toole's Rule reminds us of how much we have benefited from the work of others in formulating our ideas for this book. The works of several authors and scholars served as both a source of information and inspiration in our research and deserve special recognition including Nuala Beck, Peter Drucker, Diane Francis, Jonathan Rauch, Paul Romer, Barbara Tuchman and Margaret Wheatley. Some recent writings by Peter Drucker fueled our confidence that this book was indeed worth writing. The fresh insights of economist Paul Romer led us to believe our hypotheses would, at a minimum, turn out to be more right than wrong. Barbara Tuchman, in her own brilliant way, gave us a perspective of the past which proved invaluable for writing about the future. Nuala Beck's brilliant analysis of the new economy, <u>Shifting Gears</u> (Harper Collins Publishers, Toronto, 1993), was immensely helpful in formulating the early chapters of this book. Diane Francis' work, <u>A Matter of Survival</u> (Key Porter Books, Toronto, 1993), helped clarify and shape our ideas on globalization and the role of government in the new economy. Jonathan Rauch's compelling book, <u>Demosclerosis: The Silent Killer of Government</u> (Random House, New York, 1994), was instrumental in shaping our thinking on the danger posed by special interest politics. We would like to acknowledge the work of David J. Morrison and Adrian Slywotzky of Corporate Decisions, Inc., whose concept of value migration represents an elegant and compelling way of describing the phenomenon of value in motion. We would also like to thank Joel Rosenfeld and the Strategic Planning Institute for giving us access to the PIMS Database. Finally, we are indebted to Margaret Wheatley, whose profound work, <u>Leadership in the New Science</u>, greatly influenced our thinking on the learning organization.

The errors and omissions contained in this book belong solely to the authors, but as to its strength, there are many people to thank. Among these are colleagues, clients, and friends. But a special debt of gratitude to our editor, Dale Fetherling, whose insightful recommendations, advice and, on occasion, forbearance, made this work possible. We also must thank Jerry Eastridge for stalwart support in word processing, and Candy Baxter, Lou Savary, Kathlyn Horibe and Robbie Hunt for their outstanding copy editing and editorial advice. To Paige Moody and Jack Rosenblum, who provided valuable assistance in the packaging, preparation and project management. This book has been a playground of learning for us but none of this learning would have been possible without the support and sponsorship of clients and colleagues. They have been our true teachers. Those who have been especially helpful are: Ken Chenault, Randy Christopherson, Jim Clemmer, Carlyle Crothers, Cal Darden, Bob Drummond, Frank Erbrick, Alexandra Golinkin, Harvey Golub, John Hagerman, Joe Kielty, Jim Kelly, Jon Linen, Gerry McDonough, Art McNeil, Joe Moderow, Oz Nelson, Morris Perlis, James Robinson III, Tom Ryder, Terry Smith, Andy Somers, Bonnie Stedt, Cal Tyler, Tom Weidemeyer, Clinton (Bud) Yard, and Tommaso Zanzotto.

Other important sources are to be found in our Bibliography and Chapter Notes at the end of this book.

Part I

A New Order

Born of Chaos

How queer everything is today! And yesterday, things were just as usual. I wonder if I've been changed in the night...but, if I'm not the same, who in the world am I? Ah, that's the great puzzle?
—Alice, from Lewis Carroll's
Alice in Wonderland

Chapter 1

THROUGH THE LOOKING GLASS

Wayne Gretzky will be remembered as one of the greatest hockey players to ever lace up skates. He was once the subject of a study to discover the physical traits and athletic skills which accounted for his extraordinary success. The study concluded Gretzky's success was not due to his size or physical prowess; he is neither as big nor strong as other stars in the National Hockey League. When asked what he thought made him different from other players, Gretzky replied, "Most players tend to play where the puck is, whereas I play where the puck is going to be."

If you have seen him play, you know this is true. His uncanny instinct for anticipating the movement of the puck is without equal, and has led him to being universally hailed as "The Great One."

That ability to look ahead, to discern a future trajectory, to think several steps in advance of our peers is an increasingly valuable skill in another arena, too. The underpinnings of the world in general, and business in particular, are changing so quickly that anticipating today's problems is no longer enough. We have to focus on tomorrow's.

Tomorrow's issues are tough, because as never before, the economic ground is shifting beneath our feet. Events once considered isolated foreign phenomena—an interest rate rise in Europe, or the fall of a government in Asia—now reverberate in the local economy as well, sending shudders through even the smallest businesses. Meanwhile, power here and abroad is shifting from producer to consumer...and from traditional institutions to individuals.

As a result, old business certainties are crumbling. Strategies which always succeeded, structures which always worked, products which always sold, and markets which always performed are no longer effective. It isn't that they have gone from "always working" to "always failing." Change is never that simple. Yet, increasingly, with ever-greater regularity, the old formulas and the old organizations are losing their power. We've all seen it.

Japan Inc., thought to be invincible, hits a wall, and the European "miracle" of the 1970s slows to almost a stop in the 80s. At the same time, Mexico, which balanced its budget and reduced its debt, experiences a near-meltdown, economically.

IBM, Wang, Pan Am, Westinghouse, Sears and GM, all paragons of American corporate power a couple of decades ago, stumble, or even disappear. Suddenly, little Southwest Airlines and its clones, not giant American Airlines, become the new models of aviation profitability! (AMR, American's parent company, earns more money from its SABRE reservation system than from the whole airline! *How can that be*? How can moving little bits and bytes around, which is what a reservation system does, turn more profit than flying people around the world?)

The U.S. economy, thought by many to be in terminal decline a decade or two ago, comes roaring back. In the process many Fortune 500 companies drop from the list like flies. Meanwhile, exciting new companies are launched daily and unemployment falls to 30-year lows—*yet* millions lose their jobs in layoffs.

Yes, something out of the ordinary is happening here. But what? And *why*?

Our world, like Alice's, has turned upside down. Think, for example, of the astounding speed which communism was virtually swept away. In a matter of *months*, what then-President Bush labeled "a new world order"—and Zbigniew Brzezinski more accurately called "a new world disorder"—was upon us. Now, breakdowns and dislocations are becoming more common as old rules, assumptions and institutions are swept aside. Shocks and surprises, some pleasant, others less so, will continue to be the order of the day. Yet, out of this apparent chaos, the world likely will emerge safer and richer.

Seeing a Pattern

Most people fail to see this pattern beneath the flurry of activity and headlines…or fail to see any pattern at all. The closer they look, the more confused they become.

The key is not to look closely, but from afar. If you step back far enough, you begin to see the contours of the historic changes we are witnessing. In broad outline, they are characterized by the emergence of a knowledge-based, global economy, where everything affects everything else. No person or corporation, indeed, no nation or society, is an island. None are free from global economic influences and the shifting patterns of what constitutes value. What is going on globally and what is happening in your town and your business are inextricably linked and will define tomorrow's winners and losers.

Low interest rates in the United States, for example, can cause stock prices to rise in Malaysia. Advances in wireless communications in Latin America may force a Maine mail order firm to revamp its marketing. When American homeowners decide to refinance their mortgages, they stir up a storm in the Treasury bond market. Futures contracts traded in Chicago can undermine the Japanese Finance Ministry. In short, the economic world has become integrated and, increasingly, we are all in the same boat whether we like it or not.

Meanwhile, we are undergoing a Knowledge Revolution that stands many of the old precepts on their heads. Information, not raw materials, capital or labor, is the new key to economic power. The consumer, not the producer, is becoming dominant in deciding what is produced, where, and at what price. For instance, as the flow of information grows, so does the flood of discounters, warehousers, consolidators, catalog merchants, and consumer buying guides. Already looming on the horizon: global electronic shopping.

Look around and you will see product after product being commoditized. You find yesterday's expensive mechanical calculator displaced by digital hand-held machines, so cheap you do not even bother to have them repaired. If it stops working, you simply buy another. The same is true of most electronics today, including VCRs, radios and even televisions. The same process is at work in financial services, transportation and telecommunications and most key sectors of the economy.

Today's economy is changing so quickly that it leaves little room for slow learners. On this issue, there are none but the quick or the dead.

Two Seismic Forces

This book is about two seismic forces intersecting. One force is moving us from an economy based on the nation-state to one based on global markets; the other is moving us from a manufacturing and service-based economy to one based primarily on information and knowledge.

The convergence of these two trends marks the arrival of a new era of abundance, along with a "new" consumer unlike any the marketplace has known before. Armed with access to information and global competitive options, this buyer is now at the controls. Daily, in thousands of ways, customers are using this power to drive up quality and drive down price.

The merging of these two seismic forces has tremendous, and largely favorable, implications for society as a whole, especially over the long term. We are on the cusp of a new era of abundance that signals the arrival of more opportunity, wealth and freedom. However, it will also bring more competition, more change and more challenge.

In the short term, this puts tremendous pressure on leaders and managers, in business and government alike, to perceive and keep pace with this change. Those who operate with theories, systems and structures designed for an age of scarcity are especially handicapped.

Reshaping Our Economy

The aim of this book is to explain what's happening to business and the economy, and to prepare decision makers to better grapple with globalization and the massive shifts in economic value which lies ahead. We will explain how shifts toward information and knowledge as the key sources of value are reshaping our economy and restructuring business and government. By "value," of course, we mean economic value, what consumers believe is the overall worth of a given product or service.

Value is shifting today because consumers are redefining what constitutes wealth. Such changes often begin subtly, scarcely noticed by the big players in an industry. Then the changes snowball. For example, think of how quickly digital sound systems overwhelmed analog systems; how fuel efficient cars overtook roadhogs; how cable TV cut into the networks' audience and were themselves undercut by small dish satellites. In a world where the consumer is increasingly in control, value is a *sine qua non* for economic success. Organizations unable to provide value are headed for trouble.

As the economy shifts toward a new order driven by knowledge and information, the best way to add value will be by making a product or service more knowledge-intensive. That means bringing more technology or intellectual power to bear on the output. (For instance, the output of a programs analyst or a doctor is very knowledge-intensive while the output of a laborer or a meter maid is not. Conversely, a Ph.D. who drives a cab would not be adding knowledge unless he or she figured out a way to apply that special expertise to the task.)

Adding value and knowledge are becoming synonymous. An example: Despite severe competitive pressures, the Ford Taurus was for several years running in the early 1990s America's most popular automobile. Many factors contributed to its success: superb design, customer input, quality, reliability and affordability. These factors were byproducts of adding knowledge to the design and production process. They did not happen by accident. Nor is it an accident that the Taurus of the early 1990s contained only 600 dollars worth of steel but 800 dollars worth of electronic components. In a sense, it was more a piece of information than a piece of metal.

Quantum Changes

We are experiencing nonlinear, almost quantum changes that make it difficult to predict tomorrow's business environment. However, we can make assumptions about its nature and shape based on trends which are *already shaping our economy*. Today, more Americans make computers than cars. Health care and medical-related industries are bigger than oil refining, automobiles, textiles, steel and mining *combined*. Software, practically nonexistent 20 years ago, now is a 42 billion dollar-a-year business. Employment in knowledge-intensive sectors is growing quickly, in some cases, at double-digit rates.

These facts just hint at the shift to information or knowledge-added value in recent years. There are many more signs that will continue to appear as consumers increasingly view information and knowledge as the key sources of value, or as their definition of what constitutes value, or worth, changes.

Where value moves, margins soon follow. You can see that in how America rebounded from its economic malaise in the late 1970s and early 80s. At one point, the U.S. economy seemed to be on death's doorstep. Everywhere there were industries in trouble: steel, autos, machine tools, textiles, consumer electronics. Even semi-conductors, an industry we invented, seemed destined for the scrap heap. The future belonged to Japan, not the United States.

But the U.S. economy rebounded as 25 million jobs were created. Exports boomed in the late 1980s and the early 90s. Our share of worldwide manufacturing rose an astonishing five percentage points, from 15% to more than 20%, and is *still* growing. We regained our position as the world's leading producer of semi-conductors and the world's largest exporter of goods and services. By the mid-1990s, the U.S. economy was judged to be the most cost-competitive in the world.

Shedding Our Old Industrial Base

How did the U.S. pull it off? In short, by responding quickly to a massive shift in value. Everywhere during this period, information and knowledge took on new importance. During the 1980s, the whole world was starting to shed its old industrial base and transition to a 21st century economy, but the U.S. did it faster than any nation on earth. U.S. industries added technology and improved quality. They invested more than a trillion dollars in new plants and equipment, pared costs, scrapped obsolete systems, and shifted to a new kind of economy that is rooted in changes in customer requirements and driven by knowledge and information. As we will show, this new economy is still largely misunderstood by U.S. business, government and the press.

Even as America's new economy was being born, its old economy—steel, autos, textiles, and so on—staged an amazing comeback. It is their story which attracts the most attention. However, the real news of the 80s was not the recovery of the old industries but the rise of others in which information, not capital or labor, was the critical resource. Even the resurgence of the smokestack industries was largely the result of adding value by applying knowledge and information technology.

It is no accident that as the auto industry began cautiously hiring again in the 90s, the hiring profile was dramatically different from that of the 1980s. Suddenly, a high school and college education became essential criteria for working on the assembly line. Detroit was looking for knowledge workers.

Similarly, what consumers considered value in 1980 was largely obsolete by the early 1990s. They expected different things from products and services, and they expected them delivered faster and at lower prices.

Music audiocassettes, ubiquitous in 1980, were largely obsolete by 1990. The demand for dedicated word-processing machines in 1980 was incredibly high, but 10 years later, a floppy disk containing a word-processing "program" had virtually eliminated the entire industry. "Bank teller" became a job category under siege as did the all-purpose travel agent and any middleman who could not add unique knowledge to the value chain. So, at the heart of America's competitive turnaround was this: *information and knowledge had taken on new importance as sources of value.*

The shift from an analog to a digital knowledge-driven economy is transforming our definition of what constitutes value. Like a mighty vortex, today's value is being pulled inwards and commoditized. This commoditization process signals the beginning of an age of abundance. Once at the center of the vortex, value does not disappear, it becomes abundant. A product becomes commoditized when its availability is so great that it must compete primarily on price. Even as old value is being commoditized, it is being replaced by new, largely knowledge-driven value. We are transitioning to a new economic paradigm, in which **availability**, **affordability** and **information** are changing the nature of economic value.

As a result, value is moving in new directions and taking on new forms. In industry after industry, customers' expectations regarding a product, service or even entire industries are changing, setting off a scramble to restore profits and reexamine strategies.

Companies everywhere are running a race with shifting value. In many industries, quality must improve and prices reduced every year, just to stay even. Those who cannot keep up, find their products and services commoditized in a flash.

To cope, corporate America is restructuring and reengineering itself into a frenzy. Millions of jobs in old-line businesses are being eliminated. Middle managers are becoming an endangered species, and corporate loyalty, like chivalry, seems a quaint relic.

Government, slower and less adaptive, will be hard pressed to keep up. However, falling behind will not be an option. Unless governments can catch up and keep up, they are likely to be "fired" by their constituents. The huge, ponderous apparatus of central government has everywhere become economically inefficient and a hindrance to growth…it is simply too slow at "learning." There is a high likelihood government will be disassembled in the coming decade and reconstructed within smarter, more manageable parameters.

In every change, something's lost and something's gained. The coming Age of Abundance will not bring universally good news. There will emerge winners and losers because this new era, and the economy which supports it, will come with different rules. The rewards can be immense for those quick enough to recognize what is going on. They will be able to see a new world order taking shape that will be as different from what it replaces as the Industrial Revolution was from the Agricultural Revolution.

Counter to Conventional Wisdom

Why and how is all this happening? Where will it end? How can you thrive amidst the changes? We will try to shed some light on these questions. *Be prepared*, though, as much of what we say will run counter to conventional wisdom. For example, the U.S. economy is not getting weaker but stronger. The world will see democracy grow while governments shrink. For corporations, adding value and exceeding customer expectations will take precedence over slashing costs. Knowledge will replace raw materials as the source and object of production. As the cost of producing wealth drops dramatically even as the speed of production increases, we will find ourselves in an Age of Abundance, not sentenced to live in a world of scarcity.

How do you cope with change of this magnitude? For starters, do not stand in the way! Position yourself and your organization to move with value, not against it. Lay a foundation based on information and the commercialization of knowledge. Heed the imperatives of abundance, which are outlined in Chapter 12.

Thus, the future is not a complete mystery. New value is taking shape around us every day. Few generations have been so surrounded by opportunity. However, like Wayne Gretzky, we need to look at where the puck is going, not where it is. Clues for doing just that are on display *if* we know what to look for.

*What concerns me is not the way things are, but rather
the way people think they are.*
        —Epictetus, Greek philosopher

Chapter 2

THE NEW ECONOMY: A VALUE-DRIVEN KALEIDOSCOPE

There is precedent for today's economic upheaval. The world has been through two previous transformations of equal proportions—the Agricultural Revolution and the Industrial Revolution. This revolution is driven not by food production or machinery but by information. Call it the Information Revolution, or if you wish, the Knowledge Revolution.

In the Agricultural Revolution, land and raw materials were the keys to wealth. In the Industrial Revolution, capital replaced land and raw materials as the key to economic power. Today, knowledge is increasingly that key.

The very definition of wealth has changed. Three hundred years ago, wealth was associated with owning land and domestic animals. Today, Bill Gates, the founder of Microsoft, owns little in terms of land or factories and, so far as we know, the only animal he owns is a dog. Yet he is one of America's richest, most influential people.

Revolutions are disruptive. Each of the previous economic revolutions exerted tremendous pressure for change. That change ultimately overwhelmed the status quo, creating new institutions and new elites. Outdated technologies, ideologies and political structures were cast aside or swept away. This is precisely what is happening today.

The Knowledge Revolution, what futurist Alvin Toffler calls the Third Wave, marks the end of the dominance of manufacturing. Now, value is created by the ability to put information to work, to commercialize knowledge.

The Knowledge Revolution has rearranged the factors of production.

13

Information Revolution Value Inputs

IMPORTANCE ↑

1. Knowledge

2. Capital

3. Labor

4. Raw Materials

Knowledge is now the most important factor in raising productivity and adding value; raw materials the least important. This explains why natural resources generally are 20% less expensive today than in 1980, 50% cheaper than in 1950, and 80% cheaper than in 1920.

Capital, though important, is generally abundant, at least for jurisdictions that make money welcome. Labor also is readily available, but, as we will see, the type of labor required by the new information economy differs markedly from that of the older Second Wave service and industrial economy.

Heart of the New Economy

The microchip drives the Knowledge Revolution as powerfully as the internal combustion engine drove the Industrial Age. "The heart of this new economy is the tiny microprocessor, the transistor-packed silicon chip that combines with clever software and laser optics to make possible what we glibly call the Information Age," wrote John Huey. "The microprocessor has been around for more than 20 years, but its power has been increasing exponentially, and it now has become an essential, affordable, ubiquitous fixture in our lives."

Imagine you receive one of those greeting cards that plays "Happy Birthday" when you open it. After it brings a smile to your face, you casually toss it into the wastebasket. Huey reminds us that "you've just discarded more computer processing power than existed in the entire world before 1950."

In fact, computing power doubles every 18 months and is now 8,000 times less expensive than it was 30 years ago. This staggering increase in productivity is having a profound impact on our economy.

Historic Threshold

So much has been written about the Information Age that it seems almost like old news. In reality, the line separating the Second Wave and Third Wave economies has only recently been crossed. It was in the early 1990s that American business began spending more money on information technology than on all other forms of capital investment combined—all the machinery needed for services, manufacturing, mining, agriculture, construction and the like. This represents an important and historic economic threshold.

It means we will see the importance of highly skilled knowledge workers rising as that of low skilled production workers declines. This process is under way and explains part of the growing pressure on the blue-collar middle class.

Today's most valuable employees are well educated knowledge workers. They no longer "mass produce" things. Instead, they provide service by bringing knowledge and technical expertise to bear on their work. In this new economy, workers are less likely to tie themselves for life to factories or large corporations as they did in the past in exchange for economic security.

Even the term "worker" is becoming obsolete because many knowledge workers are really individual contributors to the wealth-creation process. More and more "workers" are choosing to contribute in ways other than full-time employment.

The contingent workforce, which includes many knowledge workers, now numbers over 40 million in the United States. This group— temporaries, part-timers, the self-employed, and consultants—has grown 57% since the 1980s. People are learning to care for themselves and their families by planning their own careers and building their own retirement funds. By the turn of the century, it is likely that less than half the work-force in the developed world will be holding conventional full-time jobs.

The new knowledge worker is less concerned about amassing possessions because those are more readily available than in the past. Instead, workers today seem more intent on making a difference in the world and adding value to their work. Generation "X" may turn out to be the most entrepreneurial Americans ever.

As the economy shifts to this new order, there will be an increasing emphasis on adding value by adding information based technology. As that technology moves "downstream," impacting not just the way something is made but how it is distributed and used, we will find higher and higher ratios of value-added knowledge being applied to products and services.

Where value moves, profits soon follow. Those industries with the highest ratios of knowledge workers and commercialized knowledge to invested capital, will command the highest margins and pay the highest salaries. Those with low or declining knowledge-value ratios will find margins eroding and pay scales declining. Already, we can see software profits creeping upwards as hardware profits decline.

Bombs, Cars and Airplanes

Bombs, though not on everyone's shopping list, provide a classic example of applying information technology to enhance performance. In World War II, "dumb iron bombs" (as they were called in the trade), guided by little more than gravity, were lucky to land within a mile of their target. To compensate, planes had to drop tons and tons of bombs over each target. In fact, it took 9,000 bombs—that's right, *9000!*—to guarantee that one of them hit within a 100' by 30' target area. In Vietnam, by contrast, it took only 400 bombs to accomplish the same task.

Today, bombs made intelligent by adding laser-guidance, self-adjusting fins, and optical-tracking mechanisms—all communicating via a battery of silicon chips—can be aimed with unbelievable accuracy and reliability. The target that took 9,000 bombs to hit in World War II and 400 iron bombs in Vietnam now can be hit with two. Two bombs...one target...one hit! And with a drastic reduction in civilian casualties, to boot. During the Gulf War, for example, laser-guided bombs accounted for 8% of the ordnance but were credited with hitting 50% of the strategic targets.

The saga of the bombs tells us a lot about the shape of the future economy. The iron and explosive in the "dumb" iron bomb constituted 90% of the raw materials in the product; the guidance packet in the modern bomb amounts to less than 10%. The bulk of the value is, of course, in the guidance packet. The information and intelligence added by the laser-guidance package exponentially increases the effectiveness of the total system. One "smart" bomb cost 20 times more than its "dumb" cousin, but is 400 times more accurate and effective. The difference in price and performance is entirely made up of knowledge or intelligence value-added.

If you were in the market for bombs, which bomb would you buy? Would you worry that it was more costly? No. You would see that the bomb's inherent value is not in its physical form but in the essential information it carries. In the civilian economy, consumers are increasingly thinking the same way.

For example, look at the automobile. Detroit, slow at first to respond, has taken the industry into the Information Age. Forty or 50 microprocessors sit under the dashboard of most new cars today. (That compares to almost none before 1980.) Microprocessors control all the operations of the engine—fuel mixture, air flow, fuel flow, timing, spark firing order, and transmission. Computer chips control the pulsing of anti-lock brakes, the leveling function of the air-suspension system, and shut down the fuel pump if the car is hit from behind. Other computer components supply a constant stream of information, ranging from fuel consumption and fuel economy, to the number of miles till the next scheduled tune-up. Still more chips run the cruise control, work the lights, govern heat or air-conditioning, display a roadmap screen, play the stereo, and trigger warning bells, buzzers, and artificial voices.

"Think of the automobile as one big system, filled with information technology," says Joe Gorman, CEO of TRW, the world's fourth-largest maker of auto parts. The average driver is unaware of most microprocessor-controlled functions, although they make the car safer and less-polluting as well as more efficient, reliable, longer lasting, and more enjoyable. Detroit, in turn, is making more money by building fewer, but better, cars. Everybody benefits as a result of adding tremendous knowledge to what is essentially a late 19th century technology.

We mentioned in Chapter 1 that airline reservation systems, essentially a knowledge-driven process, generate more profit than flying people around the world on a billion dollars worth of aircraft. Again, that is because the reservation system is more knowledge intensive than the traditional airlines they serve. This sort of value-added knowledge is going to be the key to the new economy.

17

The New Economy Today

Though we can catch glimpses of the new economy, it is important to understand that history happens in bits and pieces. The Knowledge Revolution will not occur overnight. If the past is prologue, the old economy and new will coexist for a long while in uneasy equilibrium.

With the arrival of the Industrial Revolution, cotton and tobacco were already declining industries, but remained important segments of the Second Wave economy. Even today, as the Information Age dawns, tobacco and cotton remain important crops because people still buy cigarettes and wear underwear. With each passing day, such crops are less and less central to the future of the economy.

The "underwear" connection provides an interesting look at the application of knowledge to a Second Wave industry. Playtex, a subsidiary of Sara Lee, sells bras and panties (they call them "intimates") and does so very profitably. However, Playtex *manufactures* very little. It farms out around the world the actual making of its products. This allows Playtex to focus its energies on brand management, distribution and design, and finding out what women really want in "intimates."

Is this an example of the "hollowing out" of the American economy, a retreat from what we have always done best and what has made our economy so strong? Absolutely not. Rather, it is a classic case of following value upstream to the areas of concept and design, where higher margins are. Playtex employs more people in America today than it ever did as a manufacturer. What has changed is the type of worker it employs and the ratio of knowledge applied to the work.

Much the same is true of most of today's Second Wave industries, such as steel, automobiles and mining. These industries remain important and their Second Wave status does not preclude them from growing and being profitable. However, they can do so only by adding an ever increasing ratio of knowledge to their output.

The cyclical recovery in America's traditional economic base highlights one of the paradoxes inherent in economic growth and transition: *productivity tends to be higher in declining and mature industries than in growing industries.*

Farming's productivity, for example, has increased incredibly over the past 100 years and continues to improve, even though agriculture is clearly a First Wave relic. Likewise, the productivity of manufacturing has been growing steadily for 150 years, soaring to new heights in the 1980s and early 1990s. Why? Declining industries *must* improve productivity to survive because they cannot count on growth to keep them afloat. Only the lean can survive. (An exception is state sponsored monopolies and protected industries where, all other things being equal, service and productivity will decline even as prices increase.)

On the other hand, growth industries focus most of their attention on expanding, thus they tend to be less efficient than mature industries. Eventually, the process rights itself as new industries mature and become more productive. This is precisely what will happen over the next several decades in many new growth sectors of the U.S. economy, such as health care, telecommunications, transportation and tourism.

Where to Look for the New Economy

How do you identify tomorrow's important industries? The first step, as Canadian economist Nuala Beck wrote in her brilliant analysis, SHIFTING GEARS, is: "Find out what's growing and what's not."

Do so, and you will find some surprising trends. For example, at nearly 14% of Gross National Product (GNP), health care and medical related industries represent the largest sectors of the U.S. economy while information and communications account for 8.5%. Travel and tourism, now *the world's largest industry* and still one of the fastest growing, is rapidly expanding and has become one of America's chief exports. (Inbound tourism brings in money, just like any outbound export.) Other booming sectors include telecommunications, engineering and scientific equipment, and environmental consulting and equipment.

Another way to identify tomorrow's industries is to find out who is hiring and who is not. Electronics employment, for example, has risen a blistering 18% in each of the past several years. The entertainment business employs more people than does the auto industry.

As the new economy expands, the old is slowly receding. Among Fortune 500 companies, the number of jobs declined from 16.2 million to 11.5 million over the past 15 years even though overall U.S. employment rose strongly. (Thirty years ago, manufacturing accounted for 25% of all jobs. Today, it is 16% and falling.)

How can we be expanding and adding jobs while the Fortune 500 firms are laying off millions of people? We are in a period of transition, and the old Second Wave economy is disproportionately reflected in the makeup of the Fortune 500. As that "wave" declines, so will the percentage of people it employs relative to the economy as a whole.

Such layoffs, now as well as historically, are not a sign of a dying economy but one that is being reborn. Throughout the Industrial Revolution, two-thirds of the jobs existing at the beginning of the century were gone by century's end. However, at the end of every century, there were three times as many people at work and both the standard of living and life expectancy were higher.

Unfortunately, governments and many economists continue to religiously track the economic indicators of the old economy, such as housing starts. Forty years ago when housing construction was 7.2% of GNP, it was an important indicator of future economic activity. Today, at 3.5% of GNP, housing is far less important. The same is true of steel, autos and mining.

Tracking these indicators could easily give the impression the economy is decaying. From a Second Wave perspective, the turnaround of the mid-1990s seems little more than a small upward blip in the midst of a long-term cyclical decline.

When computers and semiconductors, communications, entertainment and telecommunications, health and medicine, instrumentation, tourism and high-tech services are tracked, a very different picture emerges. While Second Wave industries are generally shedding laborers, knowledge-worker employment is expanding briskly. Thanks to Third Wave growth industries, overall U.S. employment is very strong as of this writing.

Another statistic which can produce false readings is the trade deficit. The present deficit is exactly what should be expected when the U.S. economy is growing more strongly than most of its trading partners. That is because growing economies tend to suck in imports as well as investments. Far more important to track are America's high-tech trade figures. There the picture brightens considerably as the United States has run, and continues to run, an expanding high-tech trade surplus.

With productivity high in declining Second Wave industries and slowly increasing in Third Wave industries, the true data on the new economy indicates a boom, not a decline. The United States appears to be transitioning to a knowledge-driven, post-industrial economy faster than any country or region in the world.

The New Playing Field

To understand what is happening, it is not enough just to know that the Rust Belt industries will continue to decline while the knowledge-intensive industries will grow. That is a byproduct of a much larger economic transition involving wholesale shifts in economic power, and those shifts are occurring at multiple levels. Among the most important of these shifts are:

1. **From national to global markets**
2. **From place (geographic location) to people (wherever the customer happens to be)**
3. **From low knowledge-added to high knowledge-added products and services**
4. **From the producer to the consumer**

1. FROM NATIONAL TO GLOBAL MARKETS: An entrepreneur we know wanted to start a bicycle manufacturing firm. He liked living in the Boston area, so he established his corporate headquarters in Cambridge. However, none of his bicycles are made there, nor are any sold there. His company takes up no more space in North America than a small office with a telephone, computer and fax machine. His investment capital comes from the Near East, the bikes are manufactured in Taiwan, and sold exclusively in Europe.

That small entrepreneur is a paradigm for the future leaders in the New Economy. He looks beyond national borders for solutions to his problems. Being increasingly connected, we all must develop global solutions.

Think about it. The most pressing problems we face are all transnational in nature: terrorism, nuclear proliferation, environmental degradation, AIDS, the regulation of global financial markets. Even war—one of the original reasons nations were created in the first place—has become a transnational business as shown by Gulf War coalition and various peacekeeping actions around the globe.

It was less than 500 years ago that French philosopher Jean Bodin conceived the idea of the nation-state, and less than 300 years since it first took physical form in Europe. As the millennium dawns, it appears Bodin's theory is an idea whose time has come—and is *going*. At every turn, global economic forces are wrenching power and prerogatives from national governments, while at the same time local and regional jurisdictions are demanding more autonomy. The nation-state, so familiar to all of us as the locus of power and protection in the 20th century, is caught between powerful centrifugal forces and is being pulled apart.

The decline of national sovereignty may be a scary prospect for some. However, when we examine these centrifugal forces in detail, we find they are mostly positive, such as the present movement to open markets and bring down trade barriers. In the 1930s, the world learned the hard way the importance of trade and open markets. After a murderous run-up in tariffs—a key factor in creating the Depression—trade barriers leveled out and did not really fall significantly until after World War II when the United States led the way.

In 1940, average tariffs in industrial countries averaged 40%. By 1950 they had fallen to 24% and then to 12% by 1970. In 1990, they were down to 5%, and if present trends continue, they will be 1.5% by century's end. Arguably, the present state of global free trade is the greatest accomplishment of the post-war Pax Americana.

Each of these drops reduced impediments to wealth creation, resulting in more economic growth. As tariffs come down, GNPs rise. Global trade, living standards, and overall economic activity in much of the world has risen dramatically in the post-war era, thanks in large part to U.S. free-trade leadership.

Currently, this tradition of bringing down barriers is developing a second wind. This is clearly seen in the expansion of the European Union, the North American Free Trade Agreement (NAFTA), Mercosur in South America (Argentina, Brazil, Paraguay, Uruguay, and soon Chile and Bolivia), and proposed free trade areas in Asia and in the Middle East.

In short, free trade is changing the meaning of sovereignty. Increasingly, it is not the nation-state which is sovereign, but the global consumer.

2. FROM PLACE TO PEOPLE: Sometime in the last decade, we crossed the line separating the old producer-driven economy and a new consumer-driven economy. The shift has been sudden and jolting, almost as if a final grain of sand fell on one side of a scale, tipping the balance forever.

Political scientists long have maintained that a tyranny loses power once the distribution of telephones achieves critical mass. The same holds true for producer power in a world of global communications.

With the right information, today's consumer can buy just about anything cheaper and faster, from someone, somewhere, without sacrificing quality. How many of today's young children will really know a "department store"? Instead, they are growing up in an era in which buyers increasingly are mobile bargain hunters who use the phone, computer, fax, and even the local newspaper, to ferret out the best merchandise for the least price.

With perhaps 30 million computer users roaming the Internet looking for a deal and 160,000 more said to be joining their ranks each month, the volume of inside information available to consumers is increasing exponentially. No wonder retailers and car manufacturers are abandoning "suggested retail prices" in favor of "everyday low prices."

In Europe and South America, telephone customers are phoning the United States on specially leased lines, then rerouting to a neighboring country they wish to call. Why? Because of the outrageous long-distance rates charged by local monopolies. Once these citizens discovered it was 20-50% cheaper to place a call to a neighboring country via the United States, they went ahead and did it.

Similarly, Japanese discounters now send planeloads of "professional shoppers" to the United States to bring back goods manufactured by Japanese companies for resale at home. Such goods are less expensive in America primarily because Japan's hierarchical and expensive distribution system drives up domestic prices. For similar reasons, Japanese shoppers are ordering by fax, mail and phone from U.S. mail order houses like L.L. Bean, Land's End, and Eddie Bauer. Some of these direct mail companies are now hiring Japanese-speaking phone operators and printing catalogs and supplements in Japanese. When Austria joined the European Union in 1995, Austrian consumers immediately poured across the border into Germany and Italy to buy cars. Why? Austria's highly protected and inefficient auto distribution system resulted in prices which were 40-50% higher than in neighboring countries.

People everywhere are learning to sidestep obsolete, expensive and cumbersome national arrangements, using global communication and transportation systems to evade these restrictive economic environments. Even governments are not immune from the customer revolt. That is what Canada discovered when it raised excise taxes on cigarettes by more than 50%. Normally docile, law-abiding Canadians soon developed a passion for smuggling. At one point, Canadian officials believed fully a third of the cigarettes consumed in Canada were brought illegally from the United States, where a carton cost half as much. The Canadian government finally gave in and lowered the tax.

In addition to driving down prices, information is also lowering the barriers to entry for would be participants in the New Economy. Many of today's knowledge-driven industries do not require vast resources. Bill Gates did not need to build a factory to get started in business. Nor did Steven Jobs, who built his first computer in a garage.

With knowledge as the key element of production, the start-up process for new information industries is quicker and takes less capital. The globalization of capital markets has also helped make money readily available to entrepreneurs around the world. Capital, like production before it, is becoming increasingly democratized, at least within the developed world, and this "money" revolution is quickly spreading.

3. FROM LOW KNOWLEDGE-ADDED TO HIGH KNOWLEDGE-ADDED: The steel mill, the classic icon of the Industrial Revolution, consisted of a huge plant located near its raw materials, linked by roads and railways, and served by a mass of low-knowledge workers who needed a nearby city and its many services. Compare this massive arrangement to a single, creative mind, such as the bicycle manufacturer in Cambridge. He sits at a workstation with fax and computer access to brain trusts and databases around the world.

That, in microcosm, is a picture of the fundamental shift in the underpinnings of today's economy. Even tourism, the Third Wave sector which most resembles the steel mill in terms of capital and infrastructure, today differs markedly from its predecessor. While the old steel mill many times was exploited by its owners, unions and governments at the expense of its customers, the tourist center cannot. Why? Because even though the hotel or theme park cannot move, the consumer can. If the owner's greed, the union's intransigence, or the government's taxes raise prices and lower the value for the customers, today's tourists, equipped with information and mobility, will simply go elsewhere. The Industrial Revolution, as we saw earlier, raised the value of raw materials as an essential ingredient of production. Today the hierarchy of value is reversed. Raw materials are at the bottom of the list, people are on top.

4. FROM PRODUCERS TO CONSUMERS: For business, this is perhaps the most important power shift. Consumers are now calling the shots, and there is no point fighting it. This shift is a *fait accompli*, a done deal. Consumers, not producers, are in control of today's economy and are using their power to drive down prices and raise quality standards.

To see the power of this new consumer in action, just look at the software industry and the Internet. While most software vendors were watching and waiting for Bill Gates' next move, millions of individuals signed up for access to the Internet without waiting for Microsoft to provide them with an interface. The next versions of operating systems software will support all the standard Internet services, yet none of the big vendors were directly involved in defining these new standards. The consumers effectively set the standards by going ahead and showing what they wanted from the Internet.

What we may be seeing here is a subtle but important shift in power away from software producers to individual computer users. History shows that once users take control, they never give it back. It happened in the transition from mainframes to minis and from minis to PCs. Now it appears to be happening again in software.

It was not always that way. In the days of the Agricultural Revolution and the Industrial Revolution, first the landed aristocracy and then the industrialists held sway over the economy. It was a seller's market. In those days, inventing a better mousetrap meant you could expect the world to beat a path to your door. Inventors and builders were the heroes of human progress, and the paragon of the Industrial Age was Henry Ford.

Ford was a revolutionary who set out to make affordable automobiles. His thinking was typical of the times. It did not begin with the *customer*; it began with the *product* Ford decided to make.

Products, not consumers, were the center of the economic universe. Consequently, Ford focused primarily on the means of production. His brainchild, the assembly line, changed the world as profoundly as any methodology ever invented. It allowed him, and others, to turn out large quantities of reliable, inexpensive goods.

The Model T was the marvel of its age, and more important for the long run, it democratized the process of production by increasing the availability and lowering the cost of manufacturing products. Today we think of mass production as old news, but during the age of the Model T the capacity to increase output and decrease costs mystified and astounded observers and dramatically raised living standards.

Nonetheless, demand in that era usually exceeded supply. Ford and other manufacturers could not make as many cars as could be sold. The factories were enormous and consumed huge amounts of raw materials and machinery, which often could not be provided quickly enough.

Although production was democratized, capital was not. Few entrepreneurs outside the power elite had access to investment capital. Thus, leveraging debt was a strategy available to very few.

In the 1980s, as the Industrial Age waned, power shifted once again, passing from producer to consumer. Part of the reason for this shift was the democratization of capital. Another was the growing availability of proprietary information. Easy access to such data signaled some of the first stirrings of the new Third Wave.

For many decades, restricted access to production information hobbled market activity. Even other producers often lacked access to their competitors' costs, prices and performance. That began to change with the advent of the Information Revolution in the 1970s. For example, *Consumer Reports* became widely available and revealed the price and performance of just about every product and service. Suddenly, knowledge once restricted to a few insiders became widely dispersed. This changed people's perspective of worth.

From the perspective of today's savvy customer, it seems almost quaint that consumers once regarded, for example, one brand of gasoline or one kind of laundry soap as distinctly superior to another. Competition, like information, was limited. But, no longer. Today, value is the cornerstone of brand power.

What's It All Mean?

Our economy is in the midst of a revolutionary transformation. Economic power continues to shift both vertically and horizontally. Horizontally, we are moving from an economy based on the nation-state to one based increasingly on global markets. Vertically, we are moving at blazing speed from a Second Wave manufacturing-and-service based (analog) economy to a digital Third Wave economy based primarily on information and knowledge.

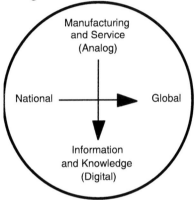

Emerging from the vortex of these two high pressure economic systems is the new consumer. Ready access to information and global competitive options have put the modern consumer at the center of the economic universe. Consumers are using their power to raise quality and drive down prices.

This relentless pressure from customers to improve performance and lower costs is forcing industry after industry to restructure, reengineer and rethink their business. In such an environment, leaders must extract the most value from their total production and distribution system. Whatever seems to be adding the least amount of value to the customer is being squeezed out.

In some industries that boils down to ripping out the middle. In retailing, transportation and financial services, the "middleman" is being eliminated. In other cases such as health care, for example, Health Maintenance Organizations (HMOs) are using their influence or control of the customer to force changes across the whole spectrum of their industry.

They add value by forcing down prices, improving medical results, and simplifying distribution.

So, like a great kaleidoscope, the North American economy is re-making itself, taking on new shapes and hues each month, each week. In the course of this metamorphosis, the nature of value is changing and moving in new directions. It is an awesome process to behold.

Part II

Value in

Motion

The universe begins to look more like a giant thought than like a great machine.
        —*James Jeans, astronomer*

Chapter 3

WHAT CAUSES VALUE TO SHIFT?

Like a powerful river carving its own path across the landscape, economic value twists and turns as customers redefine what they need and expect. Modern leaders, much like the riverboat pilots of Mark Twain's day, need to keep a seasoned eye out for snags and fickle currents.

Sometimes the shifts in the stream of value are relatively slow and steady, allowing the perceptive organization time to prepare. Just as often, value veers abruptly, leaving the unprepared hard aground at a spot which a short while ago seemed so safe and serene.

Again and again, just when an industry thinks it has perfected a product to satisfy customers, consumers find a different way—faster, cheaper or both—to meet their needs. Consider Xerox's rude awakening.

As CEO David Kearns described in his book PROPHETS IN THE DARK, the firm felt it was doing fairly well in the 1970s and early 80s. Xerox was profitable and productivity was growing by 7-8% a year, until new Japanese products began selling for less. That got Xerox's attention.

Kearns sent out teams to analyze the competition from top to bottom and was shocked at the results. The Japanese were able to carry six to eight times less inventory because they were so much more efficient at getting products out the door. While Xerox was proud that 95% of its incoming parts were error free, the Japanese figure was 99.5%. Xerox's overhead was double that of the Japanese as was its ratio of managers to workers. Worse yet, Xerox discovered that its industry was "targeted," meaning it was one of the sectors Japan, Inc., intended to dominate.

"There was no gap, there was a chasm" between Xerox and its rivals, Kearns said. Though Xerox had been getting feedback for years about the Japanese, the firm had been in denial. This startling wake-up call began Xerox's long road to competitive recovery.

Caught by Surprise

Xerox's story is not unique. Value is shifting and reshaping itself so quickly these days, it can easily catch organizations by surprise, especially successful ones. Companies structured to excel in one situation find themselves at a serious disadvantage when a value shift occurs.

Airlines like Pan Am, Eastern and TWA thrived in a regulated environment, but were entirely unprepared to cope with the low cost, competitive world of deregulation. The U.S. machine tools and consumer electronics companies were utterly unprepared for the low price, high quality, build-share-at-any-cost onslaught of the Japanese in the 1970s. The larger U.S. television studios, which dominated the entertainment scene for decades, were good at catering to the "mass middle." However, when segmentation began eroding this constituency, the "Big Three" networks fell behind the value curve.

When Xerox dominated the copier market, during what Kearns called its "fat and stupid" days, it viewed value with an inward focus. Value, in effect, was what Xerox said it was. For example, Xerox provided outstanding service to clients. When something broke, Xerox was always there to fix it, and maintenance contracts became an important source of revenue. When design or production workers discovered glitches, there was a tendency to push the product out into the market anyway, secure in the knowledge the company could always fix it later. This is a classic example of being seduced by one's own strength.

Then along came Canon. Its strategy was to build copiers that did not break down and required little maintenance, and to sell them cheaper. Overnight, the value equation in the industry turned upside down. This new value reality caught Xerox completely by surprise and before long, the firm began a long, scary decline that took it to the brink of oblivion. It was at this moment of crisis that Xerox became open to learning again. That willingness to learn ultimately paved the way for a remarkable comeback under Kearns' leadership in the 1980s.

Value = Quality/Price

Xerox got into trouble because the industry wide perception of value shifted, and Xerox was not ready for it. The lesson here is an important one. The *customer*, not the corporation, determines value. Value is the subjective assessment which the consumer and the market make about the overall worth of a product or service. Value moves in new directions when a critical mass of customers redefine what they are willing to pay for. The customers' expectations change regarding the product, service, or even the entire industry, and these shifts can happen quickly.

For example, foreign cars, with their small size, stick shifts and fuel economy, were viewed as amusing by Detroit in 1970. Consumers believed otherwise, and by 1980, the foreign makes had stolen nearly 30% of the market. This switch was based not only on quality but on price as well.

Customers see value when their expectations are met or exceeded at a cost which appears reasonable. A great product at too high a price has little value; conversely, a poor product at a very reasonable price also has little or no value. Consider this tag line: "*Our product doesn't work but it's cheap.*" Would you buy it?

$$VALUE = \frac{Quality}{Price}$$

A successful product or service must meet both quality and price criteria if it is to provide value. With consumers increasingly in control, organizations must master both sides of the value equation. If they can not, they are headed for trouble.

A short 20 years ago, the producer was in control and, in most industries, defined value. Many automakers were saying, in effect, 'We know what is good for the American people. Choices and options are what they want and we will increase our prices for every new feature we offer in a vehicle.'

Today, value is primarily defined by what the customer says it is. Those same automakers today listen attentively as American consumers describe what they want in a car, what they expect as standard features, and what they will pay.

This represents a major break with the past. Auto manufacturers, and others, are seeking what the consumer wants and is willing to pay, while producers adjust their costs accordingly. The days of cost-plus pricing are over.

The 'Black Hole' Effect

Value is a moving target. As customers' expectations rise and their preferences shift year by year, they alter the definition of what constitutes value. What satisfied a majority of customers last season may not satisfy them now. Today's delight becomes tomorrow's expectation and the following day's commodity.

As expectations rise, innovations are drawn toward a "black hole" where they are soon regarded not as breakthroughs but as bare minimums. The unique features of the first Apple computers, which made them so easy to use, are taken for granted today by most consumers. Anti-lock brakes and dual air bags, once considered expensive options on luxury cars, are becoming standard features on most automobiles. Shortly, auto buyers will expect side impact air bags, too.

Black Hole Effect

Even as the value of various features moves inward toward the "black hole," a second, even more profound shift can occur. Take computers, for example. Today the power, speed and versatility of computer hardware is increasing exponentially as prices continue to drop. This illustrates a classic "black hole" process in which old value erodes as performance improves.

This is not the only movement in value impacting the computer industry. Industry wide, value and margin are also shifting away from hardware altogether and moving toward software, indicating concurrent, multiple shifts in value.

Today, economic value is decided in the customer's mind and simultaneous shifts in value are becoming common. This means organizations, if they are to avoid being taken by surprise, must be actively looking and listening for hints of value on the move.

Too Slow to React

Examples like the rise in popularity of foreign cars seem obvious to us now, however such shifts are less easy to see from close range. Today's market leaders are often slow to react to changing perceptions of value. Like IBM when the value shifted away from the mainframe and toward the personal computer, these firms continue to maintain their primary investment in the old order, the old technology, the old corporate structure. They continue to lose vitality because they fail to recognize or understand the nature of the value shift that is happening before their eyes.

Sometimes organizations are so focused on combating the "black hole" effect, trying to protect a single product or category, they fail to take note of the far larger, more important secondary shift of value across the whole industry. Ironically, those who are not current market leaders may enjoy a distinct advantage when value shifts. Not as wedded to the old ways, they may be more able and willing to move when value shifts.

History shows that the customer base gravitates toward disequilibrium while a business seeks equilibrium. In other words, the customers tend to come and go while the company and the product tend to stay the same. This can be a fatal dynamic when value shifts. Value bleeds out quickly when the link between the company's offering and the current customers' need is broken.

The Whole Value Proposition

The bundle of value that an organization delivers to its customers is called the "value proposition." More than just the product itself, it includes price, service, selection, and intangibles such as image and brand equity. The value proposition, in short, is not just what the customer is buying but what he or she thinks she is buying. Thus, an American Express Gold Card is more than a charge card, and a Lexus is not just another luxury car.

Sometimes exceptionally strong brand and/or corporate equity can act as a bulwark against value erosion. This rear guard protection can only stall the inevitable decline, it cannot stop it.

Harley Davidson is a classic example. During the late 1970s and early 80s, when Harley was experiencing serious quality problems with its motorcycles, its distributors and customers grumbled, but stayed loyal. This loyalty, based on Harley's mystique, bought the company time to improve its quality and ultimately regain leadership in the industry.

If Harley's brand equity had been weaker when it entered the crisis, it would not have survived. Many companies do not have strong brand equity to fall back on in a crisis. A value shift can strike them quickly, fatally.

What Causes Value to Shift?

Value shifts for many reasons. Sometimes the shifts are due to epic detonations, such as major technological breakthroughs, or even wars and natural disasters.

The great advances made in post-war aircraft were a byproduct of the incredible investment made in aviation during World War II. The Cold War arms race accelerated space exploration and that, in turn, spurred electronic miniaturization. The discovery of printed circuits turned the vacuum tube into a museum piece in a matter of years. The combustion engine retired the horse as the chief means of transportation, a position it had held unchallenged for two millennia.

Not all shifts in value are so dramatic. More often, the change takes longer and is less obvious. Such shifts are no less powerful in their ultimate impact. Some of the most important and common causes of value shifts include:

Demographics

Look at the impact an aging population is having on health care, travel, housing and even clothing styles. As the baby boomers age, push-up bras, fanny-lifting jeans and relaxed fit pants are coming into fashion.

In health care, the pre-World War II generation is causing a boom in home care, ambulatory and convalescent care. As that generation retires and moves to warmer climates, it also helps push down housing prices in the Northeast and raise them in the Sun Belt states.

The aging of the pre-war and baby boom generation will also have a profound impact on financial services. As the baby boomers inherit their parents' accumulated assets, we will witness the greatest generational transfer of wealth in history. This will create immense demand for financial planning services and new financial products. In fact, this has already begun.

Technology

Technology has proved again and again that it can redefine what is possible in terms of performance and quality, as illustrated in the America's Cup race. An old sea chantey says of sailing ships, that "sailor's dreams and wooden beams are what makes them go." Today's high-tech matchups are as much a battle of super-computers as a race between boats.

The skill of the crew is still vitally important, but more and more, the margin of victory (*i.e.*, source of value) is determined by how information is brought to bear on the design and operation of the vessel. This is a microcosm of what is happening in our economy as a whole.

Closer to the average consumer's heart, examine today's new generation of semiconductors enabling computers to do things with sound and visuals undreamed of only a few years ago. This new capability is spawning powerful, innovative software. Computers have transformed information into a wealth producing asset comparable to capital and energy.

Even the normally conservative industry of banking is being revolutionized by technology. Arguably, technology is now as important to banking as is capital. U.S. banks are consolidating at a furious pace in order to acquire the financial muscle to acquire the technology which, in turn, will improve their ability to reach the customer.

When the smoke clears, it is predicted that there will be 20 or so big, technologically strong banks able to deliver a wide range of financial services to customers all across the country. The importance of branch banking will fall precipitously.

New Materials

New materials present an entirely new way of doing things. As the price of wood goes up, for example, the use of cheaper and often stronger alternatives such as steel frames in construction, is increasing. Fine ceramics are being used increasingly in engines and electronics. High-performance plastics and composites based on carbon fibers are transforming the auto and aerospace industries.

In 1979, the annual volume of plastic produced in the United States overtook steel for the first time. Plastics are often lighter and stronger than metals and can be made more cheaply. All plastic cars and planes, held together by new superglues, could be common in the next century.

Better microchips made from gallium arsenide promise further leaps in computing power while fiber-optic and satellite advances are transforming telecommunications and medicine. Cement has even gone high tech and is being used to make bottle tops, brake shoes, and loud-speakers!

Economic Cycles

Economic cycles can explosively shift value in new directions. During the Depression, value shifted away from private industry to government, especially the federal government.

The recession of the early 1990s fundamentally changed the value equation in many industries. Retail discounters and mass merchants like Sam's and Circuit City grew dramatically. Why? Their value proposition, based on large selection and low prices, was well matched to the times. One study looked at the commercialization of 112 major technological innovations and found that many were bunched in the middle of major world depressions.

Regulation or Deregulation

Changes in the rules can completely change the definition of what constitutes value and what is acceptable in the marketplace. The United States leads the world in environmental technology because the government forced us to do it. Electric cars are coming. Air bags are here already, and now that they are a standard in all cars, watch how quickly manufacturers figure out ways to make them more effective, efficient and less expensive.

In the years following the deregulation of transportation, prices fell 29% in air travel, 20% in trucking and 40% in telecommunications. The increased competition brought on dramatic changes in what customers were prepared to pay for these services. In short, the value equation was fundamentally altered. The present bold deregulation of telecommunications will have a profound impact on value propositions within that industry. These shifts in value will in turn set off waves of restructuring and reengineering.

Social Attitudes

Nuclear power is much cleaner than coal or oil and may be cheaper to produce. Yet, even such environmental and economic advantages could not save the industry from being buried beneath the public reaction to a single catastrophe. Since Three Mile Island, not a single nuclear power station has been built or commissioned in the United States. Such attitudinal shifts change what people expect in products and the prices they are willing to pay for them.

Another social preference, the desire to work at home rather than in an office, has changed the meaning of "going to work." This, in turn, has created a whole wave of new needs and caused value to move toward products and services (such as fax machines, modems and voicemail) to support home offices and attendant lifestyles.

When Americans travel to Europe today, they expect to use European cash machines. The public has come to expect seamless, highly convenient, global financial services as part of the overall value proposition—and they will get what they expect.

New Methodologies

Like new technology, new methods can raise the bar on performance. Almost a century ago, mass production was a new methodology which changed the meaning of economic value. Total Quality Management and lean production are only two of the more recent methodologies which have altered the economic value equation.

A significant new methodology can rarely be exploited without changing the basic business model which surrounds it. If a company can, by reorganizing itself, produce a better product in less time and for less money, they have changed not only the name of the game, but the game itself. For Motorola in the radio business and IBM in the mainframe and punch-card business, it was not just technology that needed to change in order for them to follow the movement of value in their industries. They needed to organize themselves in a new way, configure their resources in a new way, and perceive their customers in new ways.

Competition

Competition, perhaps more than anything else, can quickly trigger a value shift because some competitor, somewhere, is always ready to introduce new systems, products, offerings and very often, lower prices. Within the last decade, for example, two forms of inexpensive, almost instantaneous forms of mail service have appeared, fax and e-mail. They have changed the very concept of correspondence and made the traditional postal service seem like "U.S. Snail."

Now that we are increasingly part of a global economy, there are more competitors entering the market every day. Thus, there are more potential value shifts caused by competition. Thanks to global competition, automobile quality is largely an accepted given. Today, an American automaker cannot just say, "Buy my car because it's a high quality product." Quality is now expected, but this was not the case a few years ago. Until the early 1980s, American automakers could build shiny cars of mediocre quality and still easily make money. Global competition changed all that.

Shifting Values in Action

Any number of factors can set a value shift in motion. Anything which changes the needs, wants or expectations of consumers can trigger the process. Probably no industry so clearly reflects the impact on value of demographics, changing social attitudes, and new technology as the automobile industry.

Despite a strong economy and relatively low interest rates in recent years, Americans have been slower to buy new cars than most industry experts expected. Sales are up, but not by as much as the industry might have hoped during an upturn in the business cycle. Why?

There is a whole range of reasons, beginning with demographics. Women are playing an increasingly important role in car shopping. Women very often select or strongly influence the purchase of the "family car," and because so many are working, they are also buying their own vehicles. This has tilted purchasing priorities towards safety and economy because women generally see cars more as tools than as toys.

Women are also shifting home expenditure priorities back to home improvements. Both men and women now see purchasing a computer as more important than purchasing a new car. Many things are now seen as more important than a new car, including entertainment systems, new kitchens, and vacations. Owning a new car has dropped from third on the list of household priorities in 1984 to 11th in 1994.

Social attitudes also have changed. Having the latest model is not the status symbol it once was. Many people consider keeping a car and getting the most out of it as a sign of being a smart consumer.

Technology is also influencing this behavioral shift. Today's cars are better and last longer. There are also, thanks to a boom in leasing, lots of good second-hand autos on the market. Finally, the price of automobiles has crept ahead of household incomes. Contrast this with the price of electronics, which have fallen relative to incomes. With the average car costing twenty thousand dollars or more, people are taking their time before making a decision to purchase.

All in all, this is a potentially important change in perceived value. Priorities are shifting and so is purchasing power. Arguably, value has been shifting out of the auto industry for years. Automobile manufacturing is no longer as important to the economy as it was 30 years ago, and the change in consumer priorities seems part of a long-term trend.

This example highlights the paradox which often accompanies changes in value. Even as the perceived importance of owning a new car declines, U.S. auto manufacturers are doing fine. Companies like Chrysler and Ford, having lowered costs, raised productivity and improved quality, experienced record profits in the mid-1990s. This was accomplished not by selling more cars, but by selling better cars, which cost less to build.

Technology vs. Methodology

Technology is the most visible factor that can kick off a value shift. Interestingly, technology tends to follow value shifts as often as it initiates them. It usually lags rather than leads the movement of value.

Very often, when you look at the big picture, the "revolutionary" new technology cited as the catalyst for change is usually not so new. More often than not, it has been around for a long time, but no one has figured out how to use it to add value for society. The electric motor and the steam engine existed well before Henry Ford's mass production system finally gave us the means of exploiting them.

Having the capability to do something new does not necessarily mean the world is ready and willing to do it. Federal Express' "Zap" mail failed, not because the methodology was weak, but because the demand was weak. There simply were not enough people who perceived value in the product.

If technology is not a primary detonator, what is? Often, it is the methodology that organizes the technology, although the incubation period for new methodologies can be long. Total Quality Management, for example, needed 10 to 15 years, and a lot of economic pain, before the methodology took hold in North American business. Computers have been around for more than 40 years, but we are only learning now to really combine them with expert systems to dramatically raise productivity and service. Consider the value shift to home health care just beginning to blossom. Much of the medical equipment needed for home care has been available on K-Mart shelves or in mail order catalogs for a long time.

Now that the shift is finally underway, money and brain power will flow into this sector along with more and better technology to support remote health care. When this new technology arrives on the scene, it will add further to home health care's value. This new technology will be in response to the fundamental shift in value rather than a cause of it.

The new source of power is not money in the hands of a few, but information in the hands of many.
—John Naisbitt

Chapter 4

WHAT'S SO DIFFERENT ABOUT TODAY'S VALUE SHIFTS?

The movement of value is not unique to the 1990s. Value shifts occurred at the time of the Crusades, with the building of cathedrals in the Middle Ages and the rise of urban centers in Europe, with Christopher Columbus and the great age of exploration, with the invention of Gutenberg's printing press and the Protestant Reformation, with the American Civil War and with the arrival of mass production. All of these events, and hundreds of others like them, marked the beginnings of value shifts in economic history as society's needs and wants changed.

What is different today is the speed with which value shifts occur. Velocity is clearly increasing. Why? Chalk it up to two things—*information* and *competition*. There is more of both at work in today's economy.

Added competition means customer expectations are constantly being raised with new offerings. Access to information means customers quickly find out about these new possibilities. Information and competition combine to make shifts in value quick and inevitable.

Consider an aggressive investment company which pioneered "no load" funds and helped revolutionize investing. Fidelity outmaneuvered many of the old market leaders by offering a new value proposition based on cutting or reducing brokerage fees. Fidelity demystified investing and to some extent democratized what had once been a "high brow" business, catering largely to the wealthy.

Now, Fidelity itself is the subject to the scrutiny of an army of well-informed consumers. For example, Mutual Fund Investors Alert (MFIA) publishes a Fidelity Profit Alert under the banner "*Find Out What Fidelity Doesn't Want You To Know*." This means any perceived

43

weakness in a Fidelity fund is instantly communicated to the marketplace. Fidelity is now running to stay ahead of the consumer revolution it helped create.

A Nuclear Chain Reaction

Value shifts come in waves. Think about what is happening today in transportation, telecommunications, entertainment, health care or tourism. They are all undergoing massive waves of change. The pattern is clear. New expectations and needs bring on new technology, methodologies, product offerings and a host of new competitors. These factors feed off one another, igniting yet more value shifts. Taken together, the whole process resembles a nuclear chain reaction, releasing enormous intellectual energy.

The sudden shift in power from producers to consumers has unleashed forces around the world, rapidly altering value equations and causing industries to collide as they drift into each other in pursuit of value. Telecommunications, for instance, is getting involved in the cable business, and cable in the telecommunications business. Together they are venturing into the entertainment business, even as electric utilities toy with the idea of becoming information carriers.

Value is moving in a number of new directions all at once. This makes it doubly difficult, but doubly *important,* to stay ahead of the curve.

Productivity Paradox

To fail to stay ahead of a value shift is to risk becoming irrelevant. Because margins shift along with value, those organizations which catch this wave can profit handsomely. Some are so well positioned vis-à-vis the new value equation, they can make money in spite of themselves. Arguably, this is what happens in the early days of most new industries.

The new value proposition is always more efficient and more compelling than the model it replaces, and with such an advantage, profits are nearly unavoidable. For example, in health care today, value is shifting rapidly toward "integration" and "lower cost settings." This means that HMOs and home care operations are well positioned to make money.

However, these profits hide an inherent paradox. Despite their profits, these early winners are not necessarily efficient, at least when compared to the potential efficiency of the new paradigm. Take, for example, the first transoceanic jetliners. They were much more efficient and many times faster than the passenger ships they replaced. Their cost and convenience were so superior that they swept the great fleets of ocean liners off the seas in a matter of a few years.

Was the Boeing 707 or DC8 really an efficient aircraft? By yesterday's standards, yes, but not by today's. Loved by the pilots who flew them, these old jets were nevertheless noisy, smoky, gas guzzlers. Today's profitable HMOs and home care operations are health care's DC8s, better than what they are replacing, but not nearly as good as they are going to be.

This "productivity paradox" is typical of industries experiencing an influx of value. They make lots of money, not because they are efficient compared to what is possible, but because they are efficient compared to what exists. In ironic contrast, industries experiencing value deterioration and its inevitable byproduct, margin pressure, are usually very efficient. These mature industries have learned to squeeze every last ounce of efficiency from the old paradigm as a matter of survival. The only way to hold capital in the old industry, while margins are declining, is to become very efficient.

Falling into Place

Once a value shift clearly begins, vast amounts of resources follow. Look at how fast value is shifting toward home health care and how much access to money there is for companies involved in that business. When you look at that value shift in retrospect, you wonder why it took so long for it to happen.

First, home is where people prefer to be, especially when they are sick. Most people consider even the best hospitals as awful places. Second, it is so much less expensive to lie in your own bed. Third, as any nurse will tell you, you are safer at home than in a hospital. You are much less apt to develop infection or be otherwise injured in your own home than in a hospital.

There are limitations to home care, but most of them are technological. Some procedures performed in hospitals cannot be done at home. Over time, the resources chasing value will bring on an arsenal of home health care products that will change our view about what can be done at

45

home versus what must be done in hospitals. Only a few years ago testing for pregnancy required a visit to the doctor.

When a value shift like this seems so clear, one can imagine medical equipment manufacturers thinking of all the hospital products that could be repositioned for home use. (If they are not, they *should* be!)

The value shift to home care does not mean hospitals are going to disappear, nor does it mean there is no need for improved equipment or that hospitals will stop ordering equipment. There will be an increasingly higher margin in home care and pressure for medical manufacturers to create equipment to support this shift in value. As mentioned earlier, technology more often follows than leads.

In an information-driven economy, power moves downstream toward the customer, so those who are closest to the customer are best positioned to win. This is precisely what is happening in the pharmaceutical industry today. Not long ago, the real value in pharmaceuticals came out of research and development labs. While new products are still vitally important, power has shifted toward those with information on the client. Managed care companies (HMOs) began collecting information on what drugs individual patients were using, knowledge formerly held by doctors and druggists and not readily available.

Companies like Medco used this information to press doctors to use less expensive but equally effective alternative drugs. Their knowledge of the customers overtook the pharmaceutical company's knowledge of chemistry. This triumph is evident in margins which shifted toward managed care companies. In 1987, HMOs, using the services of Medco and similar firms, commanded discounts of 11.3% versus 1% for traditional buyers. By 1992, HMO discounts were up to nearly 27%. Along with this shift in power came a massive shift in market share. Managed care grew from 25.5% in 1987 to 55% in 1992 and is still growing.

Recognizing the importance of this shift, Merck & Company bought Medco in 1993. Merck's intent was not to vertically integrate (Medco does not sell Merck products) but to gain access to Medco's database. In short, it was pursuing knowledge-driven margins, which had already started to shift toward customer information.

Once value shifts, everything else falls into place, forced into a niche, or maybe into oblivion. A mad dash ensues to see who can capture the most value in the new domain. This is true of all value shifts, not just in health care. Why do you think IBM so aggressively pursued its 3.3 billion dollar purchase of Lotus? It was pursuing value, which is shifting toward software.

All in all, the process might be messy, but it works, and is fascinating to watch.

Micro *Versus* Macro *Shifts*

Economic value, as we have seen, is measured by how well a product and its price consistently meet the customer's needs, expectations and preferences. This definition gives rise to two types of value shifts. First is the *macro* value shift from a traditional product to a new product, from black-and-white televisions to home-theater units, or from typewriters to computers, for example. Although you can purchase an excellent typewriter very cheaply today, few people are interested. IBM Selectrics, once a technological marvel, now are considered relics. Second is the *micro* value shift within the same product line from one brand to another. For example, the major long distance telephone companies compete with each other, using every imaginable marketing medium and sales pitch.

When all competitors offer the same quality, price may be the deciding value factor; when all offer a product or service at the same price, then quality becomes foremost. If both price and quality are equivalent, organizations may differentiate themselves by adding additional features or services or by investing in corporate or brand equity.

This race for competitive advantage is detonated by shifts in value. Each shift sets off a commercial response, which, in turn, detonates further shifts in perceived value.

Double Shifts in Value

Value often moves in more than one direction simultaneously. Such double shifts in value can sometimes act as a smoke screen, making it difficult for executives to isolate and understand the importance of events taking place around them. In the mid-60s, passenger shipping companies, for example, were battling a shift in transportation value from ships to jet planes. When crossing the Atlantic or the Pacific, people increasingly preferred the speed of air travel (10 to 20 hours) versus the luxury of sea travel (5 to 10 days). Steamship marketing executives wracked their brains to find ways to fill berths. They lowered prices, added new shipboard activities and even tried painting the ships different colors, but nothing worked.

Meanwhile, value on a larger, industry wide scale was shifting towards cruising. Not many people wanted to cross the Atlantic by ship, but they did want to take vacations in sunny locations and going by ship was increasingly popular. Cruising, which would eventually become the fastest growing segment of the tourism industry, was born. This birth went unnoticed by most of the traditional steamship companies because their best brains were absorbed in trying to get people back on the North Atlantic. It was left to outsiders, like Carnival Cruise Lines' Mickey Arison, to lead the new industry toward the 21st century.

IBM was also taken by surprise by a double shift in value. In the late 1970s and early 80s, much of its energy was focused on the value movement from the mainframe business toward the PC business. IBM was well positioned in both businesses, but its historical roots and its chief source of revenue came from mainframes. To push aggressively ahead with PCs would threaten the old business. While wrestling with this dilemma (unsuccessfully, as it turned out), it failed to recognize the far more fundamental shift in value toward software and away from hardware altogether.

As Ross Perot likes to point out, when he started EDS, software and related services represented only 10% of the total revenue of the multi-billion dollar computer industry, hardware accounted for the rest. To IBM, who dominated the hardware sector, software looked like a side show. Yet to Perot, with a thousand dollars in investment capital, and a dream, 10% looked pretty good. IBM eventually got the message but not until later in the game. Then it had to buy its way in back into the market.

Getting Closer to the Customer

Nearly all of the value movement we see today is toward global service and value-added information. If an organization does not head in the same direction, it risks being left behind, caught in the wrong economic quadrant when the smoke clears.

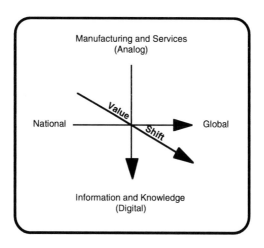

In the mid-1990s, Ross Perot's old company, EDS, now one of the world's largest systems integrators, began buying consulting firms. Why would a firm whose role is to manage a client's computer hardware and software want or need to buy a business consulting firm? One answer is to get closer to its customer.

Applying computer technology has become a key part of strategic planning and decision making. The line between consulting firms which provide strategic support services and system integrators which provide information technology services is blurring. Consultants traditionally help executives address fundamental business issues, and increasingly, information technology is one of those issues. By acquiring consulting expertise, the system integrator gets closer to the vital need driving the purchase of information technology services. It is a classic knowledge-driven strategy.

Using retail shopping as an example, in half a century, value has shifted from the small local store, to the large downtown department store, to large superstores in the malls, to today's highly segmented retail market of discounters, specialists and superstores. Where will merchandising's value shift to next? It is already happening in home shopping, which combines merchandising with the telecommunications, cable and entertainment industries.

This is similar to what is happening to personal computers for the home. Not long ago, most industry experts believed businesses would be

49

the market for powerful PCs. Yet, the home computer is emerging as the "muscle machine" of the 1990s. Today's multimedia entertainment and educational software require lots of computing power. As a result, a typical multimedia home PC now comes with a 500-megabyte hard drive. In 1994, nearly 18% of home computers were sold with Intel's most powerful chip, the Pentium, compared to 15.6% of business machines. Nearly 70% of home computers sold in 1994 had CD-ROM capability. Home PC sales are expected to surpass total business sales in 1996. This shift in raw computing power to the home, combined with the increasing importance of networks like the Internet, will only accelerate the underlying economic shift in power from producers to consumers.

Transportation is another area where knowledge-added value is bringing businesses closer to the consumer. The deregulation of transportation in the 1980s triggered a competitive free-for-all which produced a new definition of transportation value, requiring answers to three questions: How fast? How reliable? How affordable? For people on the road or in the air, travel schedules had to become instantly available. For those wanting to ship goods or documents, it did not matter if the items went by land, sea or air as long as the process was quick, reliable and affordable.

Suddenly, information became the key to adding value. For package and document transportation, customers demanded to know, "Where is my package right now and when will it arrive?" Today, any shipping company which cannot track a customer's parcel is dead. Next-day, or two-day, delivery anywhere in the country is now something we have come to expect. Rapid delivery is no longer a value added element, or a "*wow*!" factor. The value added element of logistics now lies in simplifying the process for customers and in dramatically reducing the costs. (Global transportation costs per pound have dropped, yet shipping bills in many cases have gone up because our expectations have risen, and we opt to pay for expedited delivery.)

Transportation companies are no longer calling the shots as much as they are heeding the wishes of their clients. In a sense, they are leaving the business of transportation and becoming consultants-purveyors of knowledge, expertise and most importantly, information.

The Value Chains

While executives understandably tend to focus on reconfiguring their own firms, they often overlook how the industry wide chain of value is changing. What is a chain of value? At the corporate level, it is the series of steps taken to add value for the customer, such as raw materials, items added by the assembler and the distributor, and after-sale service. Taken together, these all comprise the corporate chain of value.

It is important to understand that when value shifts, it often does so on an industry wide basis. For example, the end of the Cold War altered the value equation in the aerospace industry. There was a significant drop in demand for military aircraft. This forced dramatic changes in the way McDonnell-Douglas, Boeing, Hughes, Lockheed and Martin Marietta operated. The firms slashed costs, reduced defect rates, simplified operations, contracted-out peripheral functions, and trimmed product lines.

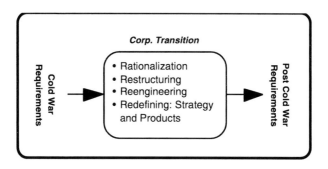

Those changes occurred within the context of individual corporations, makers of aluminum, composite materials, landing gear, simulators, windows, seats, storage bins and a thousand other items were required to reengineer their operations to stay in tandem with their largest customers. This, in turn, affected their suppliers, and the process cascaded down through the industry.

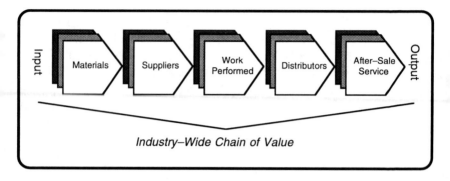

Industry–Wide Chain of Value

The tumult did not end there. It was not long before the big players in the aerospace industry began to merge operations to further cut costs. The coming together of Lockheed and Martin Marietta is a classic example as was the merger of Grumman and Northrop. Before long, the whole industry wide chain of value, from suppliers to manufacturers to distributors, was again overhauled.

Integrating the Chain of Value

Such large scale revolutions include the merging and integrating of strategic work flows across the entire chain of value. Re-engineering and integrating the "total" value chain can reveal enormous waste and redundancy.

Consider what has happened to the auto industry's chain of value over the past 15 years. First, there was rising customer expectations of quality and the introduction of lean production and TQM. As a result, the Big Three slimmed down and systematized operations. People were laid off, contracts renegotiated, and inefficient or redundant facilities closed. Next, billions were spent on new technology, new plants and state-of-the-art equipment. Huge investments were made also to train employees and more importantly, to teach employees to play critical roles as partners in a total quality process. All of this took place at the corporate level.

Meanwhile, industry wide, the Big Three entered into alliances with competitors, such as Ford with Mazda. Chrysler absorbed American Motors and its Jeep operations. Lean production and TQM meant being more efficient by, among other things, shrinking inventory. Shrinking inventory meant forcing suppliers to ship parts just-in-time, and with dramatically higher levels of quality and reliability.

That, in turn, forced suppliers to overhaul and reengineer their own operations to meet these demanding new criteria, who ended up putting pressure on their own suppliers.

Thus, the shift in value in auto manufacturing in the 1980s worked its way into related industries, such as transportation. Just-in-time manufacturing created a wave of demand for reliable, expedited transportation. UPS and Federal Express found themselves as critical links in this new, faster, leaner chain of value, because unless the goods arrived in time, the whole process broke down.

Viewed from the perspective of the total chain of value, much of this improvement was focused on the middle of the chain *production*. And it worked! The quality of U.S. automobiles shot up. Efficiency improved, in some cases dramatically. Suddenly, Chrysler emerged as the lowest-cost car producer in the world.

What about the front and back of the chain? The next stage of the improvement process requires auto executives to look downstream at distribution, which accounts for 30% of costs. It is no accident that GM set out in the mid-90s to overhaul what was called its "large, unwieldy dealership and distribution network." This process is now under way and will result in a distribution system that is cheaper, faster and more customer focused.

Information Holds the Key

Inputs → Suppliers → Work Performed → Distributors → After–Sale Service

System Integration Across Industry–Wide Chain of Value

INFORMATION

Edwards Deming was right, "the system will do what the system will do." To effect change, we must alter the system. This rule is as true today as when Deming first enunciated it 50 years ago. What has changed is our view of what constitutes the system. Increasingly, competitive advantage is derived by rationalizing and improving the total industry wide value chain. If you look carefully, you will see that this is precisely what price and quality leaders like Wal-Mart, Ford and Motorola are doing today.

Again, the key is to integrate with suppliers, share information and procedures to make the value chain transparent and seamless. Linked by common information systems and procedures, the various partners in the chain begin acting organically, as if they were one entity rather than separate companies. The result is that huge chunks of work flow are exposed as redundant and thus, expendable. It is not unusual for these reengineered value chains to be 30-40% cheaper, faster and more reliable than the fragmented systems they replace.

Top of the Food Chain

The two reengineering efforts, corporate and industry, often start simultaneously. Again, most people understand the corporate shift but not the larger one. Think of it this way: *as value shifts, so does the process by which it is delivered.* In fact, it is hard to think of a value shift which does not impact the value chain in some way.

As we have seen, large scale restructuring is taking place across whole industries. Retailing, telecommunications, entertainment, transportation, health care, pharmaceuticals and utilities are all undergoing massive changes in response to value moving in new directions. Weak players and under-performing components are being eliminated, and industries reconfigured to provide more value, quicker, and at less cost. As non-value-added components and redundant steps are replaced, the need for inventory, working capital and personnel services drop, often dramatically. Those most at risk, whether organizations or individuals, are those furthest from the customer. Those closest to the customer and the customer's need for information are most likely to be at the top of the food chain. All this movement, from the restructuring of an entire industry to the reshaping, creation or elimination of individual jobs, is set in motion by a shift in customer perceived value...a very small explosion leading to a very big bang.

Part III

Coming to Grips

With Shifting Value

In Business

When faced with a choice between changing and proving there's no need to change, most people get busy on the proof.
—*John Kenneth Galbraith*

Chapter 5

WHY EVEN SMART FIRMS SOMETIMES ACT DUMB

People, organizations, products, services and value propositions…all have a beginning, a middle and an end. Most companies last only a single generation, and only a handful make it beyond two generations. Of the 1925 Fortune 500 list, almost all are gone. Even the Fortune 500 list of 1970 has lost more than half its members. Death, as we are so often reminded, is part of life.

Although nothing lasts forever, organizations can extend life by continually adding value. Arguably, this is the only way to extend life in a free market system. Of course, this means continually adapting and changing. Unfortunately, most organizations, when faced with the need to change, choose instead to perish.

Value often shifts in one direction as the firm moves in another, much like a drowning person who, becoming confused, swims away from the lifeboat. To understand this pathology, we must first understand the lifecycles of organizations. Such cycles bear a remarkable resemblance to lifecycles in nature. Natural scientists tell us that life follows a predictable pattern, resembling a great S-curve.

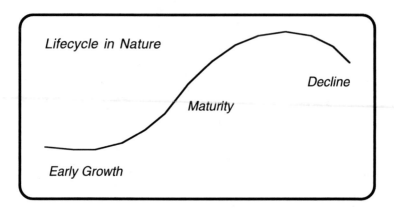

Under a microscope, these large lifecycles actually appear as multiple S-curves.

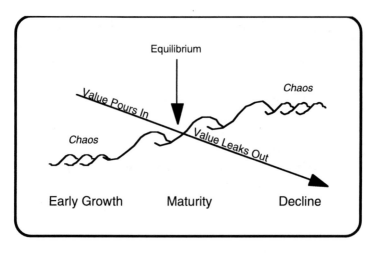

At the beginning, the short, choppy S-curves represent the pain, exhilaration and chaos of birth. The beginning of each corporate lifecycle is also shown by short, choppy S-curves. At this stage, value is pouring into the industry. From a distance, these short S-curves appear symmetrical, even aesthetically pleasing, but the truth is far more brutal. These little curves represent chaos.

Living through such periods of change brings to mind the Chinese curse, "*May you live in interesting times.*" At the beginning of the growth curve, value is pouring into the industry like a torrent. Everyone is trying to capture as much of this value as possible, but no one is sure what will work best. Consequently, multiple models, technologies and methodologies battle for supremacy. You may remember when 30 brands of personal computers and several incompatible operating systems were on the market. That is what this chaotic start up period is like.

In this early stage, as the industry searches desperately for the right value proposition, each new corporate offering brings a market response. Winning and losing can be affected by even the smallest variables. Picking the winners and losers in such a melee is a risky business. History tells us the best technology or concept may not always win out. Witness the video battle between VHS and Beta, in which the latter was considered by technophiles to be superior, but the former emerged the victor.

This early chaos reflects the heroic, entrepreneurial age of the corporation or the technology. In these heady years, anything is possible. "Try it, do it, fix it" becomes the order of the day. Everyone feels the adrenaline. This heady start up phase, though, is usually brought to an end with a bloody shakeout, followed by industry consolidation.

During the second stage, winners emerge, the long lifecycle S-curves take over and the environment becomes more stable. Value is more or less in equilibrium. The shakeout leaves a handful of players still standing, all intent on recouping their investment.

Repeating the Pattern of Success
The age of experimentation ends, and the age of implementation begins. Industries shift from tumult to stability. During this stage, success belongs to those who can master, improve and then repeat most efficiently the winning pattern or formula. The whole organization structure, way of operating, and culture is geared to repeating the pattern of success. Continual improvement becomes a central goal. Every effort is focused on refining and making more efficient the existing model. During this period, those threatening the pattern, including intrapreneurs, entrepreneurs and other champions of new models, are shunned, perhaps even exorcised. This stability can last for years, even decades. Things move merrily along until value shifts again. This next shift brings on maturity, decay and finally, lost value.

This last stage is signaled by a crisis. Within the whirling, clanking apparatus designed to repeat the corporation's successful pattern, the level of concentration and noise is so great, no one may notice the movement of value. Financial results by their very nature are lagging indicators, and thus, often remain strong well into the downturn. As we previously pointed out, dissenting opinions often are not welcome.

Old Order In Decline

As value moves from one business model to another, it slowly unhinges the old order. Whatever the causes of the value shift, such as demographics, economic cycles, deregulation, or social attitudes, the business environment changes dramatically. Profit margins head south, and in time, investment capital flows out. Slowly, imperceptibly, the old, successful model of the past becomes less and less functional. At this point the short, choppy S-curves, so familiar at the beginning, start to reappear.

Organizations with forward looking sensors, and these are few, may pick up distant signals of trouble ahead. Most are too busy perfecting the old pattern to notice. Eventually, indicators such as customer satisfaction, market share, market valuation, and brand equity start to erode, and value visibly deteriorates. Now, the short, choppy S-curves of chaos and the resulting discomfort are evident to almost everyone. There is a nagging feeling that something is wrong, but few can articulate the problem. This is the moment of truth for the institution and its leadership. If the organization is to survive, it must now move in bold, new directions. Unfortunately, if history is any guide, most fail this important test.

A Story of Failed Change

If you go out looking for it, you will find value in the most unlikely of places. The key is to recognize it when you see it. New value often comes in forms that are often very different from the old. Take, for example, a company called Slamco, Inc., which is actually a composite of several companies.

Slamco was an industrial manufacturing firm whose core products consisted of high grade construction materials. More than a century old, this firm had a long tradition of success, but found itself under increasing competitive pressure as market share shrank and margins eroded. The traditional market leader, Slamco had propelled itself to success using a simple, but powerful formula. It sold top quality products and supported clients with well trained representatives who inspected large construction projects and wrote "free" specifications.

These specifications were very exacting and so, tended to favor Slamco's high quality, premium priced products. However, because these products were among the best on the market, the client was usually well served. All in all, the formula worked well. The company experienced decade after decade of growth and achieved revenues of nearly one billion dollars.

However, by the late 1980s, this value proposition was weakening. The quality of products throughout the industry had improved greatly during the decade. Slamco no longer enjoyed an absolute product-quality advantage. Still worse, the value added by its "reps" was also eroding. Increasingly, they found themselves in competition with independent construction consultants.

Thanks to new information technology, these independent consultants provided more detailed reports and specifications than Slamco's reps. Although the independents charged for this service, their reports were perceived as being technically superior and, more importantly, unbiased. In short, the value-added provided by both Slamco's core products and its network of reps was eroding. Value was moving away from the old success formula in a classic way.

The first people to recognize the seriousness of the situation were the reps themselves. They complained bitterly to the company about having to work harder and harder just to stay even with the competition. However, the company turned a deaf ear to their concerns. "Salespeople are always complaining," some executives said as they blocked investment in the updated technology that would allow its reps to compete with the independents.

Ironically, while unwilling to invest in technology to support their sales and service representatives, Slamco did invest heavily in new construction products, even though such products were quickly becoming a commodity in the industry. Why? Investing in construction materials was something Slamco understood and was familiar with. Investing in information technology was alien and appeared risky.

The company had always operated on the assumption that its superior products were at the root of its success. This theory was flawed.

Although high quality products were indeed part of the success formula, what really made the formula work was the network of sales reps. They provided the added value which differentiated the company from its competitors.

If Slamco had bothered to look, it would have seen this truth in the numbers. During the 1980s, as the competition closed the product-quality gap, the company managed to stay ahead of the pack. Why? Because it had a superb sales force. It was only when the value-added provided by the sales force went into decline by the late 1980s that the company found itself in real trouble. Even then, its first response was to invest more and more money in construction materials.

Amidst this melee, a small band of discontented sales reps developed a new information system for managing large materials inventories. These renegades believed future value-added would come in the form of information rather than products. They began marketing their inventory management system to large national and international clients who were responsible for managing dozens and sometimes hundreds of buildings. These clients were desperate for help and welcomed the innovation. Overnight, the demand for the product skyrocketed as sales doubled and then tripled. More importantly, for every dollar of inventory management sold, the company also sold ten to twenty dollars in core construction materials.

News of the new inventory management system spread quickly through the sales force. It was the first good news for the reps in a long time, but rather than celebrate, senior management was horrified. The response of the executives was sullen and uncooperative. They were reluctant to invest in the product, and at sales meetings, they were uncommunicative and even testy when questioned about the new system. They did not like the new product because it turned everything they had ever learned about the construction business upside down. In the end, they starved the new inventory system of funding.

In despair, the renegades began jumping ship. They took their concepts, enthusiasm and expertise to the competition. Within five years, Slamco had lost several hundred million dollars in market valuation and was sold to a competitor which had embraced the "information value-added" concept. It was a sad ending for a fine firm, slain by its own aversion to learning.

The Doom Cycle

As the Slamco example shows, both birth and renewal call for vision, courage and a capacity to undertake lots of risk. However, what is clearly different between the beginning and the end is the business environment where these skills will be applied. The chaotic environment during the early growth is very different from the comfort and certainty which prevail just before the final crisis. At the beginning, resources are few, but so are constraints. Companies, often with empty coffers and burdened by debt, feed off their dreams.

At the other end of the lifecycle, resources abound, but so do constraints. Stock analysts, boards of directors, stockholders, unions, existing strategies, investments in product lines and old technology, politicians, community considerations—all these, and more, get in the way of change. Those who feel threatened by the proposed change resist mightily. Even those not threatened, like the investment community, are likely to be skeptical.

In most corporations, when a value shift occurs and the organization attempts to respond, vested interests will try to slow or even stop the process. They will perceive it, and probably argue against it, as a risky leap into the dark.

Efforts to introduce new, disturbing market information is resisted. The dangerous data is suppressed or ignored because if it were dispensed and believed, it would require changing the organization's structure. This explains why mature organizations have such difficulty launching new businesses. The old organization imposes itself on the new business and kills it off before it can disrupt the status quo. In doing so, it dooms itself.

In his book DISCONTINUOUS CHANGE, David Nadler refers to this as the "doom cycle." Circumstances change, but the organization does not. In fact, the doomed organization openly fights change by disregarding or suppressing data which points to new opportunities or requirements. Blinded by past success, doomed organizations become cautious, risk averse, unforgiving of errors and intolerant of those who would rock the boat.

By this point in the cycle, confidence has mutated into arrogance. The middle of the organization, in particular, tends to disdain outsiders and outside ideas. This makes it difficult, if not impossible, to introduce new concepts of any sort.

These vested interests can include shareholders, who will hesitate gambling on a new, unproven product or service, and market analysts, who may criticize management if it appears to be drifting away from its core competency. An underlying company wide commitment to employees, customers and existing investment can also block the transition. It is all these factors, more than outright stupidity or stubbornness, which keep organizations from adequately responding to value shifts.

In short, the entrepreneur risks all, and consults few; the CEO affects all and answers to many. The need to limit risk and gain consensus narrows the established leader's scope for action. Sometimes, it prevents action from being taken altogether. Often the best which can be obtained is permission to play at the margin of the problem, to dabble without taking decisive action. This explains, in part, the inertia which causes organizations to freeze and subsequently perish in the face of large scale shifts in value and new customer requirements.

Another Transition Under Way

Eastman Kodak Company has been a phenomenal 20th century success story, but by the mid-90s, value was on the move. Kodak had "dabbled" with digital applications, but had not made a full fledged effort, fearful it would make the company's traditional film and chemical products obsolete.

Recognizing the seriousness of the situation, the board of directors turned to George Fisher. The former CEO of Motorola was a hard driver, famous for setting stretch goals for improvement. It was Fisher who pushed Motorola toward Six Sigma (3.4 errors per million), then thought to be an impossible goal. In his early encounters with Kodak's manufacturing executives, he was promised five-fold improvements in certain processes. In classic Fisher style, he responded, "Why not 10 times?"

Upon taking control, Fisher quickly tightened costs by simplifying some segments of the business, but he did not undertake the kind of bloodletting eagerly anticipated on Wall Street. He viewed cutting costs as an important but secondary goal. Fisher is a builder, not a cutter. Instead, the focus of Fisher's value-added strategy called for growing the company by moving into the digital era. He discovered that digital technology within Kodak was dispersed and isolated in pockets throughout the firm. He even uncovered memos from past executives censuring Kodak's investments in digital businesses and technology.

In moving towards digital technology, Fisher faced a classic dilemma met by those who would effect change in mature organizations: the new technology tends to jeopardize existing investments and customers. As Fisher pushed Kodak in new digital directions, he alienated old line "film" employees. These hard working, loyal employees, produced 90% of the company's revenue and felt slighted and ignored, given Fisher's preoccupation with digital technology. Fisher did his best to make amends by championing strategies to also expand film sales, but this was perceived as an afterthought by old line film employees.

Fisher also upset people by breaking the tradition of promoting from within and, instead, going outside for executive talent. Furthermore, he had to deal with protests from some of Kodak's bread-and-butter customers. Professional portrait photographers, for example, threatened to boycott Kodak films after the company demonstrated new products that made instant digital copies of photographs, without mentioning the importance of copyright laws. One of Fisher's new "outsiders" admitted this was an error and promised to include copyright warnings in the future.

Overall, Fisher's strategy was sound—hold on to and expand the old business while growing the new digital business. The question is, will the internal Kodak system allow him to succeed? Existing employees, customers and shareholders all have something to gain or lose in this bold effort to lead Kodak into the 21st century as a leader in digital technology.

Disruptive Technology

Professional photographers, Kodak's most loyal customers, were threatened by the proposed changes. Just as often, it is disinterest, not outright opposition, which slows the introduction of new technology. That is what happened to IBM when it considered moving into minicomputers, but its large business and government customers were not interested. This demonstrates another reason market leaders usually are not very good at championing entirely new technologies. They are too busy serving existing clients, battling competitors, and looking to expand the core product to pay much attention to tomorrow's breakthrough products and services.

There is an economic disincentive, too, for big companies to be on the cutting edge. New technologies usually under perform compared to the dominant technology in their early stages of development. However, they have a way of catching up and ultimately surpassing the old technology. By the time the market leader recognizes the seriousness of the situation, the new technology or methodology has overtaken the old, and the leader is forced to play catch up.

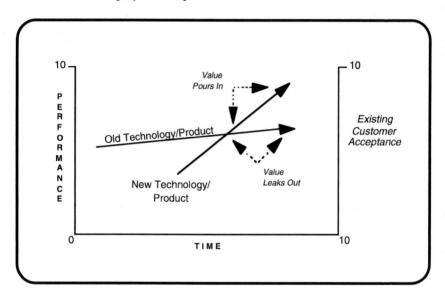

However, if you stay alert and track the movement of value, as explained in the next chapter, you should be able to pinpoint the sector of your industry that is most likely to grow. Then you have two choices: (1) become a fast follower, acquiring the needed core competencies to make the transition or, (2) buy your way in through alliances or acquisitions of smaller, nimbler competitors. On balance, the latter seems to offer the best prospects. Small firms with low overhead and a "feel" for the emerging market and technology are more likely to be successful than old line firms. It is important, though, to protect the new entity from the old, nurturing it and allowing it to be different, so it is not smothered by existing norms and procedures.

The Courage to Abandon the Old

Commercial history offers countless examples of organizations which stayed too long with an old technology or old model. By the time they realized the need to change, it was too late. Fortunately, there are also examples, although fewer, of well led companies which had the courage to abandon old certainties and move into the future.

Motorola, for instance, moved away from car radios as a core offering while the business was still strong. As Chairman Robert Galvin likes to point out, those competitors from the 1940s who stayed in the car radio business are now long gone. Motorola survived and prospered because it moved away from old businesses in time.

Northern Telecom also moved away from its core offering while it still contained considerable equity. In the 1950s and 60s, Northern Telecom was one of the world's best manufacturers of electromechanical telephone switches. Beginning in the 60s, Northern decided to go digital and develop a whole new product line based on this advanced technology. This was viewed as a "bet the company" move and opposed by many within the organization.

Although clearly a high risk maneuver, it worked. In the 1970s, Northern emerged with the DMS100, arguably the world's first affordable, fully functioning digital switch. This established Northern as a leader in digital switching and propelled the company toward two decades of extraordinary growth. As for electromechanic switches, they are historical curiosities, found today mostly in museums. If Northern had stayed with this technology, in which it had so much equity and expertise, it might have become a historical curiosity itself.

Yin and Yang of Change

In the late 19th century, American Express was a successful freight forwarder, expanding with the railways across the country. Toward the end of the century, American Express changed its core business from freight forwarding to processing money orders for immigrants. This dramatic shift was resisted fiercely by the "old railroaders." Later, the company went global when it transitioned from money orders to traveler's cheques, a uniquely innovative product which contributed mightily to the growth of travel and tourism around the world. Again, the move was resisted by powerful insiders, including many in American Express' New York headquarters.

In the late 1950s, the company again transitioned to a new paradigm by introducing its now famous charge card. It did so despite dire warnings that consumers would never give up cash for plastic. Later in the 1980s, the company again defied conventional wisdom and expanded its business to include a broad range of financial services.

This last diversification effort offers a classic example of the yin and yang associated with pursuing new value propositions. In the late 1970s, American Express Chairman and CEO, James D. Robinson III, recognized the need to move the business away from dependence on transacting money through charge cards and traveler's cheques. He and others inside the firm recognized a subtle but important value shift toward storing, or investing, money and to a lesser extent, toward lending money.

Given American Express's strong brand image, global presence, and affluent clients, the company was well positioned to provide additional financial services. In pursuit of this strategy, the company purchased a number of financial institutions, including Shearson, Lehman and IDS, a Minneapolis based financial planning firm which targeted primarily Middle America. American Express also launched the Optima Card, its first revolving credit-card, in 1987.

Timing and Execution

Looking back, it is hard to argue with the logic. The value shifts were real, and the status quo was undesirable, if not unsustainable. Despite the soundness of the assumptions, the strategy was, in the end, less than successful.

The failure had as much to do with timing and execution as it did with flawed strategy. The purchase of Shearson Lehman took place just before the downturn in the North American economy. This, combined with the speculative excesses of the 1980s, caused the market to swoon and the bottom fell out from under Wall Street in 1990-91. Suddenly, diversification into the brokerage business did not look like such a great idea anymore, and Shearson Lehman became a millstone around American Express's neck even as its Optima credit card rang up huge losses.

This all led to a transition in leadership within American Express as Harvey Golub became chairman and CEO. His approach was to aggressively pursue the existing strategy of selling off non-performing assets, such as Shearson, and consolidate the company to a core of travel related service, IDS, and the American Express Bank. He also reengineered one billion dollars out of the cost base. This done, Golub launched a host of new products, including the American Express Purchasing Card and a revitalized revolving credit product, the True Grace Card. He also rebranded IDS as American Express Financial Advisors.

By the mid-1990s, American Express again was experiencing record profits. But a careful look at the numbers showed that the fastest growing profit center in the American Express empire was American Express Financial Advisors, formerly IDS and a relic of the original diversification strategy. (IDS has been a profit maker for American Express from the beginning, experiencing after-tax earnings of 21% throughout the 1980s.) At its present rate of growth, American Express Financial Advisors will soon be generating more profits than any other component of the business.

Lessons Learned

Was American Express right to diversify in the late 1980s and early 90s as value shifted toward storing (*i.e.*, investing) money and away from transacting money? Almost certainly, yes. Remember, the worst thing an organization can do when value shifts is nothing.

American Express' longevity has been rooted in its ability to build brand strength even as it transitioned toward new businesses. The timing of this shift was clearly off and, arguably, so was the execution but the "instinct" to move in new directions was sound. This story provides a classic example of the risks associated with large-scale change—the assumptions behind the strategy, and even the strategy itself—can be sound and you can *still* get into trouble.

So Golub finds himself back at the beginning. He has record profits, cash and one of the world's great brands in his corner. Yet, he faces the same dilemma Robinson faced—a mature business whose core offering is under pressure. His initial response of launching a host of new card offerings, including a revolving credit product, looks suspiciously like an opening move. Perhaps another shoe will drop at some point in the future.

In today's economy, the status quo can never be comforting for long. As President John Kennedy liked to remind his Cabinet, "The dangers associated with bold actions are, in the end, usually less than those which accompany comfortable inaction."

Getting Unstuck Is Not Easy

It is one thing to see value shifting, but entirely another to turn this perception into an immediate, decisive and correct action. Focusing a large, complex organization on the need for change is not easy, even for the ablest of leaders.

The movement of value appears self-evident, seen from the perspective of economic history. Given enough time, distance and data, everything becomes clear. The same is true when historians dissect a long ago battle, and the necessary decisions appear obvious. However, for those involved in the real struggle, whether in the marketplace or on the battlefield, the "fog of war" is ever present.

Leaders in the midst of the fray rarely perceive "the beginning," the position from which historians later contemplate events. The great Russian writer, Tolstoy, described this reality in his 19th century classic WAR AND PEACE. In discussing General Kutuzov's decision to defend Moscow at Borodino, and later his controversial decision to abandon the city, Tolstoy provides us with what may be the best and most graphic description ever written of the chaotic circumstances in which executive decisions are made.

Tolstoy introduces us to the general as he prepares to confront the French army. He is flooded with mutually exclusive recommendations from his staff. At the same time, he cannot pinpoint the exact location of the French army and possesses only fragmentary information about the locations and movements of his own divisions. When he calls for more information, what he receives is confusing and contradictory, forcing him to use intuition to separate rumor from fact.

His adjutants, his fellow generals, the Czar, even civilians with petty gripes take up his time. All the while, Kutuzov's army continues its retreat towards Moscow on half a dozen different roads. Eventually, perhaps accidentally, the army collides with the French, and the great battle begins. Later, historians will describe Kutuzov's decision to fight at Borodino as "brilliant, courageous, an act of genius." Tolstoy knew better, and so does any CEO who has ever been involved in making decisions under pressure. Sometimes we stumble our way to success.

Leaders dealing with today's value shifts can sympathize with Kutuzov. They, too, must make decisions, often with inadequate, conflicting information amid a welter of concurrent activities. The source of the new value often poses a potentially mortal threat to the old value proposition. The leaders may intuitively sense that their old business formula is losing power, but are unsure why. Even if they do know why, the massive investment in the old system is a bar to quick action.

The Overriding Instinct

Faced with a shift in value, the overriding instinct of most leaders is to circle the wagons. The urge is to protect what already exists—brand equity, physical assets, people, products and customers. While perhaps understandable, such action can make the transition to a new value proposition very difficult. It is not unusual for executives to have a blind spot, especially in tracking the movement of value within their old core business. Data indicating a newly sprouting value can be easily denied, quietly suppressed, or sometimes unconsciously smothered to prevent it from growing and threatening the status quo.

For instance, paper manufacturers completely missed the value shift to lighter, more heat-resistant styrofoam cups. When styrofoam first came onto the scene, it was expensive...24 dollars per thousand versus 20 dollars for paper cups. It was also bulky to ship and suffered from quality problems. The paper manufacturers considered it a passing fad. They were wrong.

Within a few years, the foam cup manufacturers solved their quality and transportation problems and improved their manufacturing process to the point where they could make cups for four dollars per thousand. This spelled the end for paper cups.

Years later, the foam cup manufacturers resisted innovation in the face of new environmental concerns. One industry executive remembers hiding money in his budget to fund research and development for edible cups made from soybeans. When headquarters found out, they put a stop to it. "We're in the paper and plastic business, what has that got to do with soybeans?" And so the pattern repeats itself.

Blind to the New

A company we know was for years the dominant player in the business of making steel shafts for golf clubs. They were the market leader because they made the best steel shafts in the world, and invested heavily in steel shaft technology. Unfortunately, that heavy investment blinded them to the importance of new composite materials.

Graphite and composite material shafts were considered an amusing fad by company executives, who ignored the performance advantage of these new shafts. This denial continued even as composite shafts began to eat into their market share. Value deterioration was clearly under way, but everyone denied this reality and tried to whistle their way past the graveyard.

By this point, the company had waited too long. Almost overnight demand shifted, and composite materials took over the high end of the market. Now the company found itself faced with the unenviable task of rebuilding its manufacturing facilities and acquiring new core competencies while hemorrhaging market share and profits. With sufficient time, money and effort, the company ultimately made the transition to composite material technology, but the process was painful and costly. It would have been better to have paid attention to this shift in value toward composite in the first place.

The Importance of Change Mastery

Very often, organizations do not initially recognize value decline as the source of their problem. The symptoms can make themselves felt in a number of areas throughout the organization. In medicine, this phenomenon is known as "referred pain." A kidney problem can manifest itself as lower back pain or a high fever. It takes time, testing and experience for the medical practitioner to determine the real source of the problem.

The same is true of organizational maladies. For example, many Fortune 500 companies undertook large scale reengineering efforts in the early 1990s. They did so on the assumption they had a cost problem.

Interestingly, a number of those firms had an epiphany of sorts in the course of their reengineering efforts. For some, even while costs declined, market share and market valuation did not always improve, or improved only marginally. Why?

The market knew something the reengineers did not—that more was at work here than just a cost problem. Beneath the focus on high costs lay a fundamental erosion of value, and until this was addressed, all the cost cutting in the world would not make a difference.

The real payoff from reengineering, the firms found, came not from cutting costs, but from finding new ways to add value for customers. While paring expenses was useful and necessary, it was not sufficient to win back the marketplace. The key to victory lay in finding ways to grow value for customers and ultimately for shareholders.

Confronted with value erosion, the worst thing an organization can do is nothing. The initial response may be off the mark, but at least the organization is responding. The capacity to change and adapt to new market conditions and rising customer expectations is becoming an indispensable ingredient for success in today's economy. When value shifts, you *must* shift with it...quickly. Change mastery is emerging as a key competency for the next millennium.

Knowledge is power.
—Francis Bacon

Chapter 6

HOW YOU CAN TRACK THE MOVEMENT OF VALUE IN YOUR INDUSTRY

As discussed in Chapter 1, Wayne Gretzky's success as a hockey player comes from his ability to anticipate where the puck is going. The same is true in business. That ability to look ahead, to anticipate where value is going, is an increasingly invaluable skill in business. "O.K.," you might be thinking, "but how do you discern where it's *going to be*?" The answer varies from industry to industry. The movement of value in transportation, for example, is different from that in financial services. However, some patterns are becoming clear.

Knowledge-intensive work has become the new cornerstone of our economy. The shift to knowledge intensity is unmistakable in almost every key economic statistic: overall growth, exports, productivity, employment, margins and salaries. You name it, and the numbers tell the same story.

If you watch margin and where it is going, you can map the movement of value towards information and knowledge. Industries with the highest ratios of knowledge workers that employ the most knowledge-intensive systems are likely to be quickest at adding value. Jobs, salaries and margins are growing most rapidly in categories like software design, interactive advertising, management consulting, nursing and computer security—all of which are knowledge intensive. In contrast, jobs and salaries are shrinking in areas of low or modest knowledge intensity such as bank tellers, phone operators, factory workers, newspaper reporters, middle managers, farmers and government workers.

Asking the Right Questions

Wayne Gretzky's proclivity for anticipating where the puck is "going to be" cannot be taught in a clinic. Likewise, tracking the movement of value is not a natural inclination for many organizations, but it is not really difficult if you have the tools. Recognizing the phenomenon in the first place is what is hard to do, particularly for those closest to the old value proposition. Unless the shift is seismic in nature, it is easy to miss. Outsiders, not trapped by existing assumptions and models, have an easier time recognizing a value shift, than insiders close to the status quo. For example, a casual observer might have recognized value was shifting away from mainframe computers long before IBM insiders recognized the problem, or at least were willing to admit it.

For insiders who really want to know—and that is the key, *wanting to know*—it all comes down to paying attention. Start by asking yourself these questions:

- What do my customers value today? How is that different from yesterday?
- What will customers pay for? (It is especially important to know what will get customers to part with that last incremental dollar.)
- Which segments of your industry are growing and which are shrinking? What is different about these sectors?
- Which segments are commanding the most margin and where is margin shrinking? What is different about these two sectors?
- Whose market valuation is going up and whose is going down?
- What is happening to our market valuation?
- What patterns do you see when comparing the value propositions of those going up versus those going down?
- What is selling, what is not, and why?

Also, equally important, take time to ask your sales or service people about customer expectations. Find out if your organization is saying "no" a lot. If so, find out what it is you are saying no to. The answers may tell you a lot about where value is heading in your industry.

Competitive Scoping

Create a map or picture of your competitive landscape. This is like designing an industry specific radar screen. Set aside two-thirds of the screen for well known competitors and one-third for emerging competitors. Emerging, or marginal competitors, are companies which appear lost and have drifted into your business.

Do not be fooled by these strange looking characters. They may look odd, but they can be deadly. They are probably not lost, in fact, they likely know exactly what they are doing. They plan to smile a lot while stealing as much of the market from you as they can, hoping you are too stupid to notice. And guess what? History shows that is a pretty good strategy. Market leaders tend not to take much notice until the newcomers are at their throat. Taiwan's Formosa Plastics is now the world's largest maker of PVC, but even in the late 1980s, the major players in the industry took little notice.

Where did these intruders come from and how did they get in? *Something* changed. Sometimes, it is a new technology that opens the door. Or perhaps some change in how your product or service is distributed. Regulations may have eased, thinning the traditional walls separating industries. Or, maybe there is a new pattern of alliances in your industry that the interloper takes advantage of. If any or all of these occur, businesses can shuffle into new territory.

For example, titanium, instead of steel, is used in mountain bike and racing bike frames. Meanwhile, metal alloys, having reached their temperature and durability limits, today are being replaced in product after product by plastics and composite materials, which typically are more moldable and machinable. Many cars now have plastic body parts. A ceramic turbo engine is used in Nissan's 300ZX sports cars, and lhobham ceramic armor is displacing steel on all modern tanks.

Thirty years ago, no one in the steel industry regarded plastics or composites as a competitor. They did not even show up on the industry's competitive radar screen until well into the 1980s. Today's composite materials are competing with steel everywhere, especially in high margin sectors of the industry. From golf club shafts to precision tools, composite materials are becoming dominant.

Today, the same sneak attack is at work in banking. A host of financial service companies are establishing banking-like relationships with their customers. After ignoring this phenomenon for years, banks are finally recognizing it as a serious threat—they even have a name for it, "disintermediator." This awakening comes not a moment too soon. Already, the banks are being outflanked by these new non-bank competitors who are offering investment, checking, money transfers, and loans to customers.

These non-banking competitors are establishing beachheads in a number of important sectors, including the funding of new businesses. Banks appear especially inept at finding and floating growth companies. It is no accident that traditional banks, the chief source of capital to the old Second Wave economy, now account for only a small fraction of the money raised by corporations and individuals in the United States. Why? Because growth companies are usually knowledge-intensive. The assets are intellectual, which look suspiciously intangible to traditional bankers who much prefer collateral consisting of fixed assets such as machinery, inventory, bricks and mortar.

The arrival of cyberspace and "e-cash" will only accelerate the move away from traditional banks. How serious is the threat? The truth is that banking is required, even in a cyberspace world, but banks, as we know them, are not.

The same process is at work today in transportation. Airborne Express is competing with Federal Express, and both are competing with the U.S. Post Office's package delivery services. Meanwhile, new integrated logistics companies like Ryder are establishing alliances with key industrial customers like GM's Saturn car division. Ryder's mandate is to keep parts, people and trucks in nearly constant motion, and it uses information technology to pull this off.

For example, truck drivers plug a plastic key loaded with electronic data into an onboard computer. The screen tells them where to go, which route to take, and how much time to spend getting there. This reduces or eliminates inventory, dramatically improves cycles times, lowers error rates, and reduces costs.

The integrator becomes *part* of the host company's operation, so Saturn is now very dependent on Ryder because a great deal of technology integration and programming has been done by both parties. This means Ryder, now close to the customer, gains ascendancy over the total transportation and logistics chain of value, including the trucks and planes.

The role Ryder plays is not unlike the role a systems integrator plays in the computer industry. Systems integrators will ask for bids on hardware or software from suppliers on behalf of their clients (which forces prices down). Ryder does the same thing with trucks and planes (which also forces prices down). In a sense, trucks and planes are becoming the commodities.

The other transportation/delivery outfits are now a step removed from the customer. In time, relationships such as those Ryder is building may allow integrated logistics companies to come between Airborne or Federal Express and their largest customers.

Are You Being Invaded?

Are there any strange newcomers drifting into your market? Before saying no, think about it carefully! Is there anyone meeting a similar need, or providing a similar service, but in an entirely different way? Remember, these odd characters can be lethal. You do not want to wake up one night to the sound of a little voice telling you, "They're *here*." Now is the time to pay attention.

You can start paying attention by drawing up a competitive radar screen. Begin by drawing a simple circle on a page. Divide the circle into two sectors, one for well known competitors and one for the strange newcomers. Now, put in the names of competitors which fall into either category.

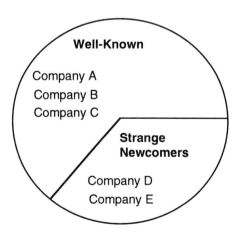

Once your radar screen is done, draw a red circle around those competitors, in both sectors, who are growing in terms of market share, revenue or market valuation. On one side of the page list those competitors that are growing, and down the other side, show those that are not. Ask yourself: what is the difference between these lists in terms of strategy, economics and value proposition? Do any patterns emerge?

Chances are that some very distinct patterns will be evident. For example, in the domestic-airline industry, one growth sector is characterized by short haul, point-to-point carriers which are mostly non-unionized and have significantly lower costs (*i.e.*, Southwest Airlines and its clones). Internationally, companies like British Airways are increasing market share and margins by taking advantage of their huge economies of scale, vast network, high service levels, lower costs and immense brand equity. Caught between the two, old line domestic carriers are weighed down with expensive hubs, high labor costs, and huge capital costs.

Growing	Not Growing	Pattern

Value rarely sits in one place for long. Where is it headed today? What are the characteristics of the winners in your industry? What patterns and processes are associated with success? How closely does your organization resemble these patterns? Do you look like one of the winners, or do you more closely resemble the losers?

Commitment to Learning

Tracking the movement of value on an ongoing basis is simply a matter of discipline and commitment. Commitment to what? *Learning!* Learning means, in short, a willingness to put aside the old ways of thinking and trying to understand how your organization really works. Learning means being obsessively attentive to customers' needs and their changing perception of value. Thus, learning holds the key to survival in tomorrow's economy.

Learning organizations do things differently. They pay attention to what is going on around them. To promote learning, they set up first rate information gathering systems to track market conditions, industry and corporate performance, employee satisfaction, technological trends, and most importantly, customer satisfaction, customer loyalty, and customer perceived value. Other important listening systems focus on brand and corporate equity, market valuation, market share and market trends.

One of the reasons firms with comprehensive Total Quality Management systems consistently outperform the market is because the TQM process forces them to pay attention to their business environment. They consistently track such things as employee and customer satisfaction, and regularly conduct performance benchmarking. In addition, companies with TQM are generally more sensitive to customer and market requirements. In short, they have learned to listen. Thus, they are more likely to detect the movement of value and less likely to be ambushed by shifts in customer sentiment. For example, the steel golf shaft manufacturer cited earlier, was considered a laggard in implementing its parent company's TQM process.

The main shortcoming of TQM methodologies is their primary focus on *existing* customers and products. Despite this limitation, TQM monitoring provides a solid foundation for building a system which can track the movement of value. The key is knowing what to look for within the stream of customer data created by the quality improvement process.

Staying Ahead of the Curve

Of course, the most important thing to remember about the movement of value is to stay ahead of it. No one can afford to fall behind the value curve in today's competitive environment. When value shifts, you must shift with it and quickly. If you are not listening for and tracking value with good monitoring systems, and responding to shifts with new strategies, you are setting yourself up for a nasty surprise down the road. If you focus exclusively on "lagging" indicators, such as income statements, to assess progress, you are already behind the curve. By the time you realize you have a value problem, the value shift has already happened.

Organizations must be able to look over the horizon at tomorrow's customers and tomorrow's definition of value. At a minimum, they must have in place a system for tracking customer satisfaction, customer perception of quality and value, corporate and/or brand equity, and customer loyalty as measured by customer propensity to recommend and/or repurchase. They also need good customer listening systems, good employee debriefing systems, brand equity measurements and cost benchmarks.

Anything less than this constitutes a case of "flying blind," no instruments, no maps, no compass, just the wind in your hair. That can be invigorating for a while, but it can also turn deadly.

The Value Landscape

Where is value moving in your industry and how fast is it moving? There are many ways to track the movement of value; some are cursory, others more thorough. Given enough data, you can draw a complete picture of value and its movement in your industry or sector. This monitoring process includes the following eight areas: margin analysis, growth analysis, stock and market valuation and industry expert assessment, brand and corporate equity assessment, customer satisfaction and perception of value and employee satisfaction, system integration and core process redesign, and economic value added or cost of capital analysis.

Let's look at these bellwethers of a value shift:

MARGIN ANALYSIS

Margin is a surrogate for value; when value shifts, margin follows. By tracking margin, you can actually "see" the movement of value in the numbers. If a product commands 20% margins in an industry which overall has margins of 5% or 6%, then something is up. The perceived value of this product is clearly higher than that of its competitors.

One large systems integrator noticed a small blip on its revenue screen. Its information security business was enjoying margins five to six times greater than its core business. The firm quickly responded to the nascent demand and now happily reports that information security is a major source of growth for the company.

Similarly, a U.S. toolmaker discovered that small Japanese machine shops were buying its high tech tools even though the company had never targeted these customers. Though the products were complex, the Japanese found them easy to repair and maintain. So the American firm, taking note of that windfall, soon became an industry leader in North America and Western Europe by specially designing products for small machine shops.

85

Margin growth, combined with overall market growth, usually points to tomorrow's market leaders. Thus, tracking the margins of both your firm and that of your competitors is vital.

If you watch where margin is going, you will find it is usually chasing value. Unfortunately, this is not what most industry leaders watch for. They tend to focus on traditional indicators of success, such as profits and market share. Those are important measures but they are "historical" in nature, telling what has already happened, not what is going to happen. Leaders are handicapped with tunnel vision when they watch these numbers exclusively.

GROWTH ANALYSIS

Who is growing and who is not? Forget about size and profitability for a minute and look exclusively at growth. Tomorrow's winners start small, but they grow fast; the key is finding them.

When the American auto industry was heading for trouble in the late 1960s, General Motors, Ford and Chrysler were watching each other nervously, when they should have been watching Toyota, Honda and Nissan. When demand for dedicated word processing machines began to level off in the early to mid-1980s, Wang, CPT, NBI and other industry leaders were competing by adding new features. Meanwhile, the DOS standard for PCs had liberated entrepreneurial programmers to develop word processing applications such as WordStar and WordPerfect which were no longer hardware dependent. More recently, another standard, TAPI (technology applications programming interface) now poses a threat to the dedicated PBX switchboard—personal computers equipped with circuit boards and software can now perform many PBX functions. Suddenly, relatively unknown firms like Dialogic, Mediatrends and Brooktrout are stepping into the ring with NEC, AT&T, and Northern Telecom. In the steel business, U.S. Steel, Bethlehem Steel and Inland Steel battled each other like three leviathans, while Nucor and Nippon Steel ran away with huge chunks of the market.

STOCK VALUATION AND INDUSTRY EXPERT ASSESSMENT

Stock valuation and interviews with market analysts who are experts on the industry can provide invaluable insights into value for publicly traded companies. Market valuation may not tell you how profitable a company is, but declining market valuation clearly signals something is up.

The stock market is a better predictor of increasing value than is a balance sheet. A company's balance sheet is a measure of capital, the amount of cash deposited by investors in the company. Whether such capital translates to value depends on how the firm is managed. No balance sheet can answer that, although, in its own crazy way, the market does.

While it may appear irrational at times, the market is still one of the best barometers of value available. It tends to discount today's profits and look toward tomorrow's profits and/or tomorrow's growth. If market valuations are low, it is because the market senses something troubling about the future. But *what*?

Perhaps the market sees intensified or even self-destructive competition, such as the airlines are now engaged in. Perhaps the underlying technology or value proposition is aging or the organization is under investing in its future. Perhaps the market senses drift at the top of the corporation. Whatever the perceived problem, such numbers could signal value deterioration, and should be treated seriously.

BRAND AND CORPORATE EQUITY

What is the state of your corporate and/or brand(s) equity? Is this equity strengthening or weakening? Very often, the inherent value of a product is rooted in its brand equity. When customers buy a Compaq computer or a Harley Davidson motorcycle or use an American Express Gold Card, they are acquiring more than just a raw product or service. There is something about the name or brand which adds an additional element of value to the relationship. When corporate or brand equity goes into decline, the perceived value of the product or the service invariably follows.

CUSTOMER SATISFACTION AND PERCEPTION OF VALUE

This is the bedrock for any value assessment. Unless customer satisfaction and perception of value is high, your value equation is probably eroding. It is that simple.

It is important to note that *satisfaction* and *loyalty* are different. Traditional quality management systems have focused on measuring customers' satisfaction with products or services, which provides important data. Beyond "satisfaction," it is important to measure "customer perceived value" and "customer loyalty" as determined by propensity to repurchase.

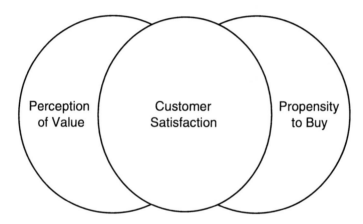

Customers may be satisfied with a given product or service and still not repurchase. Why? Because they perceive some decrease in value, as measured by the ratio of customer perceived quality over price.

In the late 1980s, Digital Equipment Corporation's minicomputer business was on a downward slope, yet in survey after survey customers rated DEC their top vendor. Similarly, in the early 1990s in the U.S. auto industry, 85-90% of customers claimed they were satisfied. Yet, the average repurchase rate held steady at just below 50%. In both cases, the information on satisfaction provided little information about repurchase decisions, and thus little about value to the customer.

Why would a customer claim satisfaction but still not have a high propensity to re-purchase? For openers, competitors may be cutting price, thus altering the value equation. Or, the brand or corporate equity of the product may be in decline, reducing its perceived value. The product may no longer be seen as fashionable or contemporary. It may lack utility or some features which are considered important. There are any number of reasons why customers may not repurchase even though they are nominally satisfied. This is why it is vitally important to track both customer satisfaction and customer perception of value.

Salespeople and other front line employees are usually the first to sense value erosion, so they can be critical sources of information. Specific survey questions aimed at them can be very helpful in picking up the initial, faint signals of changes in customer perceptions of value.

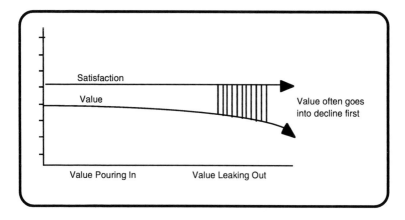

During a company's halcyon days of growth and strong earnings, customer satisfaction and value usually move in tandem. At the beginning of an obsolescence cycle, customer satisfaction can remain amazingly high even as the value begins to decline and customer loyalty erodes. If a decline in value goes unchecked, it eventually impacts satisfaction. This can take time, and in the interim, you may be dangerously exposed. By the time the dropping "satisfaction" indicators come across your desk, market share is most likely also in decline, and the damage is done.

Compaq Computer in the early 1990s offered superb quality and service. Competitors were aggressively cutting prices, causing Compaq to lose market share. By the time it woke up to the problem, its value proposition and its profits were in decline. Compaq adjusted quickly and because of its high perceived quality and brand equity, eventually won back the lost share, but at a cost. It would have been better not to have fallen behind in the first place.

Again, that is why successful businesses keep a very watchful eye on their competitors. Airline employees, for example, continually monitor the prices other airlines are charging for common routes. If a competitor comes out with a new discount package, the airlines want to be the first to know. They do not want to read about it in *USA Today*.

EMPLOYEE SATISFACTION

It is also important to track employee satisfaction. Front line employees are often the first to sense the erosion of perceived value, although they usually do not articulate it in terms of shifting value. What they see or experience are dissatisfied customers or declining sales. There is *almost always* a positive correlation between declining employee satisfaction and large scale value decline. When the organization hurts, front line employees hurt.

Harvard Business School's Leonard Schlesinger showed there is a definite relationship between *employee* satisfaction and *customer* satisfaction. In a study of an insurance company, he found that the primary source of job satisfaction was the service workers' perception of their ability to meet customer needs. Those who felt they got results for customers registered job satisfaction levels more than twice as high as those employees who felt they did not.

Whatever the source, when employees are unhappy and demoralized, sooner or later it affects the customers.

INFORMATION SYSTEMS AND CORE PROCESS RE-ENGINEERING

In a knowledge intensive environment, information technology becomes a vital asset. The ability to manipulate and move information becomes a source of competitive advantage. Information and the flow of work must be synthesized to maximize the productivity of knowledge. A key outcome of a value landscape assessment is to determine whether present work processes and information technology are capable of carrying out tomorrow's business strategy and delivering new business outcomes. All too often, the answer to this question is no. Unless these deficiencies are addressed, any new business strategy is doomed to underperform. In a world where value added and information added are becoming synonymous, a company's IS/IT capability becomes either a strategic asset or a strategic liability.

MARKET VALUATION

Calculate the market valuation of your own company and its competitors. The formula is simple enough: market valuation divided by revenue. If possible, add debt to revenue, since the money was borrowed to add value and this is one way to determine whether or not it is doing so. If you run the numbers on yourself and your competitors, some interesting patterns regarding the movement of value will likely emerge.

For organizations losing value, the implications can be profound, not just for shareholders but also for suppliers, employees and the community in which they operate. It is important, though, to note that falling into the value decline range on market valuation assessments does not mean the business is not profitable or viable. Many businesses in value decline are very profitable, but chances are they are not growing. It is also worth noting that a business can be profitable and still not earn its keep in terms of paying for the capital it uses. That is why Economic Value Added (EVA) can be a very useful tool.

ECONOMIC VALUE ADDED

EVA® is a simple, easy-to-use formula that can show if you are earning enough to justify the capital being expended in the business, division or product line? In other words, does this business pay for the capital it employs? The formula for EVA is based on operating earnings less taxes and cost of capital.

A company or an entity within a company may be profitable, but still provide low economic value. In short, it is not returning enough to pay for the capital it is using. Alternatively, a small unit with modest profits may have high returns relative to the cost of capital invested.

Sales — Operating Expenses — Taxes — Cost of Capital = EVA®

Debt or Equity

EVA® (Trademarked to Stern, Stewart & Company, New York.)
Proponents of EVA® believe that investments in quality and training should
be treated as capital expenditures and expensed over 3-5 years.

When value moves or takes on new form, the first challenge for management is finding out where it has gone and what shape it is taking. Even after this investigative work is done, organizations may find it hard to pursue the new value proposition aggressively. Why? Because the bulk of the organization's resources, especially money, remain tied up in the old value proposition and getting that money freed up is not easy. "Old" products and service offerings experiencing value decline may remain profitable. Often, they represent the core of the old business and are integral to brand equity and corporate history.

Trying to squeeze money out of these old products and services to fund new ventures in pursuit of value can be very difficult. There are always a thousand reasons why the money and resources should stay put. The hardest argument to resist involves aggressive growth plans for expanding the old value proposition. It is hard to say no to people who want to grow the business. However, we should be asking, "Is this the right business to grow?" That is where EVA comes in handy.

By using EVA, an organization can identify which product, service, operation or activity has unusually high productivity and adds unusually high value; or conversely, has unusually low productivity and is not adding value. Knowing that, you can locate capital that can be freed to chase a value shift.

Assessing performance against the cost of capital is not a new idea. It was used by Alfred Sloan at GM before World War II and later by General Electric, until the market began to focus more on earnings. The concept remains a powerful one and has been successfully reintroduced by Stern, Stewart & Company as an important management tool. Economic Value Added is being used by AT&T, Coca-Cola, CSX and Quaker Oats, among others.

One financial services firm we have worked with had a core product which had become synonymous with the company's brand image. Margins were shrinking and so was share. However, the company still had a huge chunk of its invested capital tied up in the old business.

Meanwhile, a small, fast-growing segment of the company seemed to spring up out of nowhere, selling new virtual products to the existing customer base, mostly over the Internet. Insurance, telephone services, travel specials, whatever products or services customers indicated they wanted, was sold through this new arm of the firm. With a ten million dollar investment, it returned revenues of a hundred million dollars in its second year. The small business was "virtual" because the company did not own or build any of the new products it was selling. In essence, it was leveraging other people's research and development investments. The whole business was run by a staff of 20. Next to the old giant, this new virtual business looked tiny and inconsequential, but it represented the future.

An EVA or similar cost of capital analysis would have revealed the need to shift capital from the old, dying (but still profitable) business, to the new, growing sector of the company.

Properly used, EVA can highlight areas which are inefficiently tying up resources which might otherwise be employed chasing value.

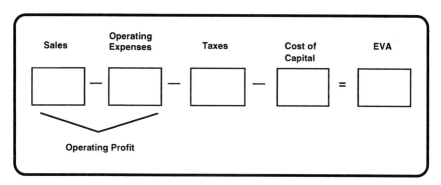

The rising popularity of EVA as a financial management tool further demonstrates the search for value in the new economy. If you want to determine EVA for your company or division, follow the formula and remember to capitalize quality and training expenses. If the number comes out negative, you may not be effectively using the capital at your disposal.

Is There Life After A Value Shift?

Do companies or industries experiencing serious value erosion ever move themselves back up the curve to value prosperity? Yes, occasionally it happens. Remember our discussion about the value crisis that steamship passenger companies found themselves in during the 1960s? One of the oldest and most traditional of these companies, Holland America Line, made the transition from crossing to cruising very successfully. It shifted its headquarters from Amsterdam to the Dutch Antilles, brought down its costs, purchased new ships, and pioneered new routes, such as to Alaska.

By the 1980s, its ships were sailing full and HAL, as it is called in the industry, was viewed as one of the most successful cruise lines in the world. Interestingly, it made this transition while preserving the best of its "Old World" traditions, including luxury, superior service, cleanliness, and superb food. HAL even advertised that particular style with the tag line "Ocean Liner Service" and made a big hit with modern travelers.

When Value Shifts, So Must Everything Else

The whole global economic apparatus is now driven by value. Consumer power, combined with increased competition and information, is a sure formula for the movement of value. As value shifts, so must strategy, structure, technology, advertising and overall service and product offerings. Such changes are not made easily or quickly, but the sooner an organization reacts, the better. Organizations taken by surprise in a value shift may find they are too far behind to catch up.

The movement of value is often transparent. To see it you must be on the lookout. Value as perceived in your customer's mind is the source of your company's economic life and vitality. The ability to recognize, measure and track shifts in economic value as they occur in your industry, provides a crucial strategic advantage to any company.

The Lesson of "Enigma"

Edwards Deming, founder of the modern quality movement, liked to point out that it was the first 15% of a process that had the greatest impact on the outcome. Get that right, and the remaining 85% falls into place.

When it comes to business, what is the first 15%? Strategic and market planning clearly fits in there somewhere. Getting your value equation right, targeting your customers, and figuring out your distribution channels are also part of the up front effort. In other words, the first 15% consists primarily of "knowledge labor," where you figure out what needs to be done and how to go about it.

It is a thinking game. It is also an information game. Once you know what to do, the remaining 85% consists of executing the plan effectively and efficiently. Both ends are important, but the first 15% has a disproportionate impact on the overall outcome.

In business today, with customer expectations growing and value on the move, figuring out what needs to be done is more important than ever. Those hoping to muddle through without planning or preparation are headed for trouble. Strategic intelligence regarding customer requirements, shifting value perceptions, cost benchmarking and competitive analysis is absolutely vital in today's environment. The payoff from having the right information and knowing how to use it is enormous. The cost of not having the right information or acting upon the wrong information is staggering.

By way of analogy, one of the most important factors in the Allied victory during World War II was the breaking of the German "Enigma" and Japanese "Purple" codes. Breaking these codes was an incredible technological achievement. To pull it off, British and American counterintelligence units worked for years and actually designed and built the world's first computer. From early in the war, the Allies knew much of what the Axis powers were planning to do, and when they were planning to do it. The importance of this information cannot be exaggerated.

Great victories, like Midway and D-Day, were made possible by the availability of vital strategic intelligence. The cost of obtaining this vital data was insignificant compared to its impact, and even more insignificant when compared to the cost of the total war effort.

By war's end, the United States alone had expended more than four hundred billion dollars in achieving victory, an incredible amount of money in uninflated 1940s currency. The United States would also spend another one hundred billion dollars rebuilding its allies and former enemies through the Marshall Plan and other aid programs. In comparison, breaking the Enigma code, which made victory possible, was financed with a budget of a few million dollars.

These figures reveal why the cost of getting the right information and intelligence up front is infinitesimal compared to the ultimate cost of executing the plan or strategy. Yet, this investment is the best insurance you can buy for guaranteeing a successful outcome. Few executives would argue with this logic, yet when push comes to shove, a great many are reluctant to make even a small investment in their intelligence gathering systems. Perhaps this is because the intelligence gathering and planning stage of the business process is intangible and a little arcane, while the execution phase involves the application of real resources—people, buildings, technology, marketing and advertising. These are forces executives understand.

Whatever the source of this blind spot (and that is what it is, a blind spot), we would all do well to remember the lessons of Enigma: *those with the best information, win.*

Man is a tool-using animal...Without tools he is nothing, with tools he is all.
　　　　　　　　　　—Thomas　Carlyle

Chapter 7

USING OLD TOOLS TO GET A HANDLE ON NEW VALUE

Because the economy and, indeed the world, is changing so fast, it is essential to keep our feet firmly on the ground as we plan for the future. The movement of value is an issue best addressed with coolness and common sense. The last thing we need is another onslaught of hype such as accompanied the debut of reengineering in the early 1990s.

Americans are our own worst enemy when it comes to novelty. We become so enamored with new ideas, we burn through them the way a child rips through toys on Christmas morning—squeals of delight, followed by three or four minutes of interest, then onto the next new plaything. That is our pattern with new management techniques, too.

We fall in and out of love very quickly. We adopt each new methodology without making sufficient intellectual investment to understand the underlying concept. Then we are disappointed when the new miracle tool turns out to be useful, but not a panacea. Not having really mastered the idea makes it all the easier to abandon as we move on in search of the next Holy Grail. That is why management fads are almost uniquely an American phenomenon.

We are inherently impatient and hunger for instant gratification. This weakness is exploited by fast talking consultants and a news media desperate for a new angle on a story. As the former Fox network CEO Barry Diller pointed out, we have a tendency to "spin subjects to unsustainable heights and then let them fall. We want everything there before the fact and when it doesn't materialize instantly, we dismiss the whole thing as impossible or a failure." In short, we set ourselves up for disappointment from the beginning.

In truth, the incubation period for new ideas takes much longer than we might like to think. The press, for example, can move the "information super highway" from concept to reality in a matter of weeks, but the real thing will take years to pull off.

Oscillating Between Extremes

New ideas and concepts take a long time to germinate. For instance, installing quality improvement concepts within U.S. industry took more than a decade. And even then, it only took hold in those sectors which were subject to intense and relentless competitive pressure.

There is no better place to view our fickleness than Business Process Redesign, or "reengineering," as it has come to be called. Re-engineering is a useful, powerful process for radically redesigning strategic work processes. Unfortunately, it was shamefully oversold and, in many cases, poorly implemented. As the inevitable reengineering failures make their way to the front pages of the business press, a predictable reaction will set in. Re-engineering will go from "hero" to "bum" overnight as process redesign and breakthrough thinking falls into disfavor.

Our propensity to oscillate between extremes, to view management techniques as either perfect or useless, is silly and gets in the way of learning. In the real world, things are rarely tidy. Strategies and tools do not always work as planned, and even when they do, the results are rarely neat and clean. In truth, the whole process of applying new techniques and tools is messy and involves a lot of trial and error.

No management tool is omnipotent. Value Landscaping™, described in Chapter 6, is a useful tool for tracking the movement and transformation of value. That is all it is...a *tool*. And no management concept or tool is a substitute for getting the basics right.

If the core product you offer is broken, there is no point attempting to realign your business around a new value proposition. If the work flows in your organization are riddled with waste and service failures, it makes no sense undertaking an arcane reengineering strategy. If customer satisfaction monitoring systems do not work, or worse, do not even exist, there is no logic in setting up elegant systems for tracking brand equity or the movement of value. The improvement process must start at the beginning, with the business plan and the basic product or service.

Getting the basics right really does matter and is certainly a pre-requisite to adopting more sophisticated or advanced improvement strategies. It is time to move beyond the hype and let common sense play a bigger role in our thinking and planning.

The Importance of Need

Before all else, comes the need to change and stay abreast of shifting customer requirements. This may sound pretty elemental, but you would be surprised how often this is overlooked or slighted. To better understand the change process, we undertook a study of a number of large, successful reengineering efforts in the early 1990s. These large scale efforts each involved targeted improvements of several hundred million to over a billion dollars. We sought to learn what patterns and methodologies worked. As consultants, we wanted to find out what change methodologies were most successful, and then, of course, replicate them for sale. Imagine our horror when we discovered that implementation methodologies were *not* central to success!

While we did find a number of characteristics common to successful change efforts (such as a clear aim, superb communications, and a focus on concrete results), these were not the primary determinants of success. The real driver of change was *need*.

In this survey of reengineering and corporate change efforts, the most important finding was contained in a single line: "*Having a compelling need to change is a better predictor of success than any given methodology chosen to drive the change.*" As we probed more deeply, it became clear that the cornerstone of change was understanding what needed to be done and believing it was necessary to do.

IBM's problems in the early 1990s, for example, were rooted in the firm's unwillingness to see the need to make the kind of painful, large scale change that new CEO Lou Gerstner ultimately had to force on the corporation. Even as late as 1994, 40% of IBM's middle managers did not perceive a need for radical change. With such a "frozen middle," it is a small wonder that previous CEOs were not able to move the organization toward reform.

Without a clearly perceived need, real or induced, it is unlikely any organization will undertake painful but necessary changes. As our survey showed, if the need was clear and the leadership present, most organizations found a way to make change happen, even if they had to grope and crawl their way through the process. Having superb implementation made the process easier and reduced the pain and expense, but that was not the critical factor for success.

Out of this study we developed our primal change model which contains four elements:

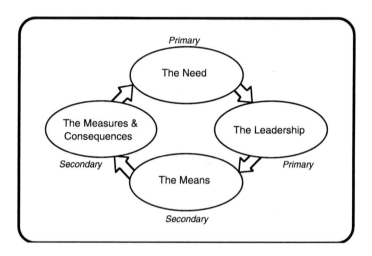

The basis of successful change begins and ends with having a clear, compelling need to move away from the status quo. Unless you recognize that where you are is not a good place to be, there is no perceived need for change.

Next comes determined leadership. It is hard to do much about the need without leadership. A high need, low leadership combination can be deadly. Without leadership, an organization which knows it must change becomes dysfunctional, or even hysterical with anxiety.

An organization which knows it is in trouble, but is offered no way out by its leadership, goes "nuts," as one of our clients succinctly put it. Turf battles break out as every sector and every individual seek to protect themselves. Common purpose and customer focus are quickly buried beneath an avalanche of self-interest. No organization can survive long in this state.

When both need and leadership are present, the next prerequisite is having the right measures and consequences. That is, the organization must be able to define where it wants to go and how it will quantitatively know when it gets there.

These quantitative measures describe what will be different after the change has been successfully made. These outcomes must then be tied to appropriate consequences. If the organization must boost customer satisfaction from 94-99%, or reduce cycle time from one day to one hour, those measures must be built into corporate plans and cascaded down through the organization. This planning only works, though, if backed by appropriate consequences. Those who achieve their goals and assist the organization in achieving its goals must be rewarded. Those who fail to make their goals or inhibit the organization in achieving its goals must be subject to some consequences. This is why most successful change usually results in turnover at the top or middle of the organization.

Only when all these elements are in place—need, leadership, measurements and consequences—should the organization focus on its change methodology. Once the foundations are in place, the organization should seek out the best, most robust blueprint for change that it can find.

Again, even the most exquisite methodology will fail in the absence of a compelling need and focused, determined leadership.

A Look at the Old Tools

In the spirit of exercising common sense, let us look at some of the tools required to manage in this new knowledge-driven economy. Value may be taking on new forms, but the tools required to manage in this new economy are not necessarily new. In fact, the most important ones have been around for a long time. We just have to learn to use them in different ways.

1. FORCING MECHANISMS

Creating a need for change is not easy if the crisis has not arrived yet, or the employees do not recognize it. Most people and organizations would prefer to wait for a crisis to clearly arrive before acting. By then it may be too late or many of the best options may be gone.

Great leaders throughout history have always understood the power and symbolism of forcing mechanisms. When Caesar landed in England, he ordered his troops to burn the boats so there could be no turning back. Now *that* is a forcing mechanism! When a Roman legion appeared in danger of giving way to the enemy, the legionary commander would sometimes resort to a strategy known as "throwing the standard." This meant throwing the legion's standard, the equivalent of its regimental colors, amongst the enemy. For a legion to lose its standard was the ultimate disgrace. Those not killed in the battle would be subject upon their return to Rome to extreme censure and possibly even death. So "throwing the standard" was one way of immediately focusing everyone's attention on the *need* to improve performance. Nothing quite so drastic as "throwing the standard" is required in modern business to focus people's attention on improvement. Most employees want to do better and require only a little direction, encouragement and leadership. History also shows that successful organizations easily fall into a state of entropy, where the impetus to improve disappears. When this happens, a forcing mechanism can jolt the organization into action.

When Jack Welch took over as CEO of General Electric in 1981, the company had backlogged orders of over 28 billion dollars, sure to provide a rich stream of revenue for several years to come. Many GE executives thought that was good enough. What Welch saw, though, was a paucity of orders for steam turbines and nuclear power equipment that augured ill farther down the road.

Welch adamantly declared that any business which could not sustain a number one or two position in its industry would perish. That was a forcing mechanism that had the effect of bringing sometimes reluctant managers on board.

Far-sighted leaders can use the measures and consequences component of the change model to force the organization in new directions. These forcing mechanisms constitute ambitious, strategic goals which are linked to appropriate consequences. Motorola's Six Sigma, GE's "One, Two or You're Out," American Express' one billion dollar reengineering target are all examples of successful forcing mechanisms. For organizations suffering from complacency or market-leader syndrome, forcing mechanisms can be a powerful tool for eliciting change.

One of the most effective forcing mechanisms is to set stretch targets for improvement, such as moving from 99% accuracy (about 10,000 errors per million) to 99.999% accuracy. Or, as Motorola did, aim for six sigma, or about 3.4 errors per million.

However, setting stretch goals will only create a compelling need for action if everyone believes the leaders are serious about achieving these aggressive targets. Forcing mechanisms must be backed by the credibility of the organization's leaders. They must make it clear these targets are real and that people will be held accountable for achieving them.

2. EMPHASIS ON QUALITY

We see headlines in the business press these days which ask, *"Does Quality Still Count?"* What utter nonsense! Despite America's impressive quality and productivity comeback, a chasm exists between where we are and where we need to be regarding quality.

Just look around. Are you satisfied with the output of public education? If quality is not a problem anymore, how is it that aircraft companies build, and the FAA approves, planes that crash when they have too much ice on their wings? Why do trains derail and spill toxic wastes, all because work processes failed or in some cases, did not even exist? What about the man who entered a Tampa hospital to have a leg removed, and woke up the next day to find they had removed the wrong one? How is *that* for a quality failure?

Or, how about the airline's hub-and-spoke system? Does it work? If you think so, try getting from New York to Savannah, through Atlanta or Charlotte on a Friday afternoon. Why is it the technical manuals for your VCR cannot be understood by anyone who is not an electrical engineer? How about those 1-800 "Help" numbers which always ring busy? Have you ever stayed in a hotel where the soap dish in the shower will not hold the soap, or the water turns scalding when someone flushes the toilet eight blocks away?

Quality as a discipline has only had a short run in this country. While we have made significant progress, we should not take our eye off the quality ball. There is still plenty of work to do. If a product or service is poor, then quality management is still not an integral part of that organization's *modus operandi*. In fact, each year American business and government wastes 30% or more of its revenue through errors and rework stemming from poor quality. That's 30% of 6.5 trillion dollars. Does quality still count? You *bet* it does.

Interestingly, most of the talk about quality being yesterday's news comes not from the board room, but from the press room. The press, in its relentless search for a new angle, has become bored with quality. And no wonder—it has been in the headlines for a decade or more.

The business press played a vital role in awakening North American executives to the importance of quality improvement in the 1980s. Documentaries like NBC's "*If Japan Can, Why Can't We?*" helped detonate America's quality comeback. The concepts of process redesign and Total Quality Management are no longer mysteries requiring interpretation and explanation. In fact, David Glass, the CEO of Wal-Mart and one of the country's most important business leaders, lists THE DEMING MANAGEMENT METHOD as his favorite book. Fifteen years ago, most Fortune 500 executives did not know who Edwards Deming was.

While quality may no longer be a novelty and no longer news, that does not mean it is no longer important. In truth, after years of hard work by both business and government, America still has a long way to go in the quality revolution. Less than 40% of major U.S. corporations have launched organized quality improvement efforts. The challenge is to get the rest of corporate America to focus on quality.

Those firms which do, such as Intel, Motorola, Ford, Xerox, Black & Decker, UPS, American Express, and Milliken, need no encouragement from the press to stay the course. They can see the results for themselves. As survivors of the 1980s quality wars, they know what happens when you take your eye off the quality ball. Having fallen behind and sweated blood to catch up, they do not intend to make the same mistake again.

So we should not worry too much about press disinterest in quality improvement. The thing to worry about is the level of business interest in the subject, and here there is still work to be done.

The New Dimensions of Quality

Quality remains the single most important component in determining value, yet the definition of quality (*i.e.*, what matters to the customer) is changing. The days are gone when having a product that merely "worked" could separate you from the competition. Compliance quality is still important, but it hardly constitutes a competitive advantage. Workability has come to be expected. So you need to find ways to add value to your workable core product or service. In today's economy, this means adding information and knowledge. At its best, this value-added knowledge enables you to partner with the customer and become an extension of the customer's business or life style.

Levi Strauss, for example, uses technology to custom fit jeans for women. The customer is measured as she tries on sample jeans in the store, then the data is forwarded to a computerized fabric cutting machine at the factory. The custom ordered jeans cost only ten dollars more than the mass-produced versions.

Similarly, the transportation industry adds value by tracking products and speeding up delivery times. Integrated logistics firms add value by remaking the host company's logistics chain and dramatically reducing costs. Charge card companies add value by providing customers with travel management services and the capacity to extract discounts by bundling purchases. Software producers add value by enhancing the capacity of the customer's hardware.

3. CONTINUOUS IMPROVEMENT AND INNOVATION

There is a lot of talk these days about the importance of product innovation and process breakthroughs. This debate reflects one of our periodic swings in sentiment away from continuous improvement, towards innovation and breakthrough thinking. Just wait, the mood will swing back again. Not so long ago, innovation and rampant individualism were out of style. We were in the throes of rediscovering the importance of standardization and the power of eliminating redundancies. We found that by straightening out the kinks in work flows, we could produce dramatic improvements in productivity. When done properly, the results were amazing…speed rose, costs dropped, productivity improved, and so did safety. It was like a miracle, people could hardly believe it.

Then along came the reengineers with their focus on "discontinuous improvement" and the pendulum swung back toward innovation. Soon, Continuous Process Improvement (CPI) appeared rather dull and pedestrian. The reengineers took advantage of this sentiment to label CPI as slow, unimaginative and mechanical. None of this was true of course, but the message suited the marketing needs of the moment. Today, with the benefit of hindsight, we can clearly see this was a false quarrel. The marketers of reengineering picked this fight because it helped differentiate them from the Total Quality Movement, and we fell for it.

Re-engineering and CPI are just different points along the same continuum. To start one is to begin the other. The polarization caused by this debate was harmful and distracting, and about as relevant to the real economy as the annual fashion debates about hemlines. The overblown rhetoric surrounding such tools as reengineering create an obstacle to learning. The supposed dichotomy between CPI and innovation was never real, at least as it applies to existing businesses. For an organization seeking to improve, it is not a case of choosing one over the other, but of pursuing one or both when they make sense. Teams which set out to incrementally improve processes very often break through and achieve dramatic results. Inversely, breakthrough teams searching for dramatic improvement often fall short and only achieve incremental results. Either way, things get better.

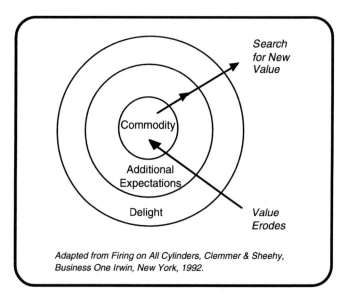

Adapted from Firing on All Cylinders, Clemmer & Sheehy, Business One Irwin, New York, 1992.

At the core of this continuum is the basic product or service. This core, although successful today, must be continually replenished and renewed to meet rising customer expectations. The core offering begins to decay from the moment it is born. The minute a product or service is introduced, competitors try to match or better it. Even where the competition is slow to respond, the product ages by virtue of its own longevity. Disneyland today offers a host of new experiences that were not available when the first Disney theme park opened. If Disney, content with success, had rested upon its laurels and not added attractions, the company's overall value perception would have long since declined.

In highly competitive markets like electronics and telecommunications, these waves of rising expectations can crest very quickly. Today, households are throwing away obsolete computers which contain 10 times the digital power Apollo 11 took to the moon. We are now discarding five million computers a year globally. Television viewers already take for granted big screen TVs and digital sound, as well as home theater systems with access to 100 channels. For those of us brought up with "*Howdy Doody*" and two channels, the pace of obsolescence is mind-boggling.

How do you stay ahead in such a fast moving environment? You pay attention to customers. Where else are you likely to find out what customers want and where the market is going? This explains why organizations with first class customer listening systems tend to stay ahead in their markets.

4. MANAGING THE CUSTOMER BASE AS AN ASSET

Some customers can tell you how to improve your *existing* products and services and how to make them better, faster, cheaper or more convenient. Other customers, a troublesome minority which is never satisfied, can provide insights into *tomorrow's* requirements and expectations. These tough, hard-to-handle customers hold the key to the future. They stretch suppliers to the limit with outrageous demands.

These unreasonable customers make a point of challenging the status quo. They are not satisfied with what you currently offer or how you offer it. They want more, and in demanding "better" or "different" outcomes, they very often take you to the limits of your existing paradigm and point the way to the future.

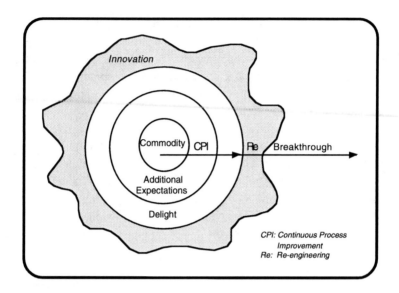

It is no accident that Michael Porter in his authoritative work, THE COMPETITIVE ADVANTAGE OF NATIONS, listed "demanding customers" as critical assets in building a world class industry. For example, American aerospace owes part of its success to the demands of its toughest customer, the U.S. Air Force. In its relentless search for lighter and stronger materials, better engines, and improved avionics, the Air Force pushed suppliers to the limit by continually upping the specifications. As a result, U.S. aircraft makers became the world's technical leaders in the industry, and this edge spilled over into the manufacture of commercial aircraft as well.

In his autobiography, test pilot Chuck Yeager described how high altitude aircraft can come right to the edge of space. At altitudes near 100,000 feet, the stars of outer space are visible beyond the earth's atmosphere, even at mid-day. Pilots who have flown to such heights have been "to the edge." This is what tough, demanding customers do for a supplier; they take you "to the edge." If you stay with them and do not falter, they will show you the future in the form of tomorrow's value. This brings you into the fourth ring of innovation where reengineering was born.

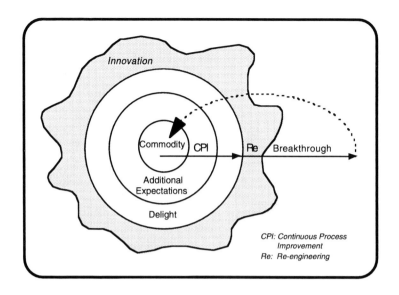

However, if you go beyond this point, you leave the realm of continuous improvement and innovation and enter the heroic landscape of the innovator or inventor. At this end of the spectrum you encounter the scientists, inventors, entrepreneurs and eccentrics who will bring us tomorrow's ideas and technology. These people are not interested in improving things, they want to *create* things. Once the new technology or innovation is created and in place, its value immediately begins to erode. You start again trying to improve the new core offering, and the whole improvement cycle begins anew.

Tough Customers As Assets

Successful companies staying abreast of the movement of value almost always have access to a core of tough, demanding customers. These customers do more than just keep you on your toes, they force you to improve. Often, they will even point the way to the future in terms of new product and service offerings. Take the case of the transportation industry. Its toughest customers are most likely to be found in the area of integrated logistics, where customers become outright partners. This explains why having a successful, growing logistics business is essential to any large scale transportation company today. Integrated logistics becomes that industry's window on the future.

109

Twenty years ago, Japanese auto manufacturers were winning over large numbers of the U.S. auto industry's toughest customers. These customers were more concerned with finding value than helping preserve the Big Three carmaker's dominance of the U.S. market. They were even willing to endure the "Buy American" ire of their countrymen to get what they wanted.

The term "learning organization" has been used to describe so much, it runs the risk of losing its meaning. Yet, if you hang around with tough customers long enough, you will soon discover what it means to learn. Tough customers force you to learn. If you do not keep up, they dump you. The key is to constantly seek out these customers, and then once you have them, do everything you can to hang on to them.

Impacting the Bottom Line

Proper management of the "customer asset" can have a greater impact on the bottom line than almost any other form of asset management. Invariably, there is a dramatic impact on net earnings if you can increase by even a few percentage points this group's propensity to buy. This explains why quality theory has always maintained that keeping rather than getting customers is the key to business success.

Frederick F. Reichheld and W. Earl Sasser, Jr., in their ground breaking *Harvard Business Review* article "Zero Defections," showed how a 5% increase in customer loyalty can produce a profit increase of 25-85%. A later study in *Fortune* showed that Reichheld and Sasser's estimates were probably conservative.

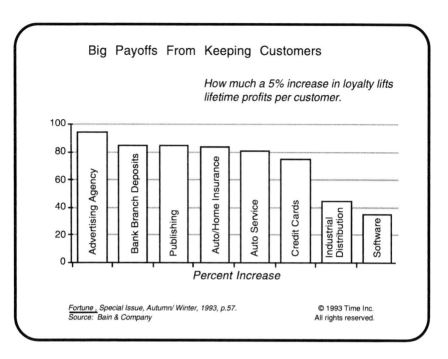

Big Payoffs From Keeping Customers

How much a 5% increase in loyalty lifts lifetime profits per customer.

Percent Increase

Fortune , Special Issue, Autumn/ Winter, 1993, p.57.
Source: Bain & Company

Although all customers are important, some are clearly more profitable than others. The most loyal customers are usually the most profitable of all. Companies that take the time to analyze the figures are likely to find their most loyal customers (i.e., the top 20% in terms of spending and longevity) account for most of their profits. Take these customers away and many corporations would find their business no longer viable.

The economics of customer loyalty was demonstrated to one financial services firm when it experienced an astounding 16% spending increase after implementing a customer loyalty program aimed specifically at long time customers. More importantly, this new spending by existing customers came in an industry where the cost of getting new customers runs seven times higher than maintaining old customers. The cost of the loyalty program, which consisted of offering incentives and frequent flier mileage points for using the product, was significant, yet it was small compared to the cost of trying to raise 16% more revenue by attracting new customers.

Customer loyalty programs can include special discounts, parties, premiums and other rewards. For example, General Motors, by launching a co-branded credit card that put 5% of spending toward the purchase or lease of a new car, was able to offer a savings to its loyal customers while helping boost its own sales.

Surprisingly, few companies monitor customers on a regular basis, and fewer still make special efforts to enhance their relationship with their most loyal and profitable customers. Sadly, many firms *do not even know* who these customers are because the companies lack a system for tracking them.

Sensitive customer tracking systems identify not just (a) customer satisfaction, but also (b) customer perceived value, and (c) propensity to buy. While these three categories are closely related, there can be subtle but important differences. A customer may be satisfied and still not have a high propensity to buy again. Understanding what drives customer behavior is essential to building loyalty and managing the long-term relationship.

Calculating Customer Asset "Yield"

In an environment of margin pressures and increasing competition, organizations must learn to manage all their assets, including the most important one, customers. Firms must think in terms of improving the "yield" on their existing customer base. This will not happen by accident. It will require a disciplined strategy aimed at enhancing loyalty and increasing the propensity to buy.

Most often, organizations do not know what the customer is really worth, except in the very gross sense of total revenue. One way of personalizing this learning is to assess the lifetime asset value of a single customer in your top 20% category, using the formula below.

One client in the medical field, after completing this formula, was astonished to find that its customers were worth several million dollars apiece. Yet another client, in the capital goods industry, discovered customers whose total lifetime value was several hundred million dollars. In the consulting business, few clients have a lifetime asset value of less than 750,000 dollars. Even in low margin industries, such as home products or cosmetics sold directly to households (such as Avon or Shaklee), the lifetime asset value of a customer can be tens of thousands of dollars. The formula* goes like this:

Average Purchase _____

Multiply by the Average Number of
Purchases Per Year _____ X _____

Total Annual Asset Value Per Year _____

Multiplied by the Number of Years Customer
Stays With Organization X _____

Multiplied by the Capacity of this Customer
to Influence at least One Other
Person to Purchase 2 X _____

Lifetime Asset Value _____

(*Derived from Clemmer and Sheehy, FIRING ON ALL CYLINDERS, Business One Irwin, 1991)

Having customer contact employees and executives complete this net asset value exercise is an extremely effective training tool. It brings on a *gestalt* that forever changes one's view of that customer across the counter or on the phone.

While it is important to know what the customer is worth, it is even more important to know how to drive up this net worth. How do you go about doing this?

Go back to the formula and ask yourself at which points you could increase the value of this customer? There are several points of leverage. For example, you could:

A) Increase average amount of purchase
B) Increase frequency of spending
C) Extend the relationship over more years
D) Increase the propensity to recommend or refer

Each of these represents a point of leverage where you could increase the yield on your existing customer base. After all, you have already paid good marketing money to get these customers into your system, so the cost advantages of this strategy are enormous.

Intimate Knowledge

The key to leveraging your company's relationship with customers is intimate knowledge of them. What sort of knowledge? Well, for example:

- What drives spending frequency and amounts?
- What actions could be taken to increase frequency or deepen spending?
- What additional value will be needed to enhance loyalty or increase propensity to spend?
- What could we do to deepen and/or broaden our relationship with the customer?
- What could we do to increase their propensity to refer and recommend?
- What additional needs or requirements does the customer have which are presently not met?
- Are there additional products or services which could be sold to this customer through our existing distribution system?

This information is readily available, given the right tracking system. Once armed with this data, it is possible to design a loyalty program which adds value in the eyes of the customer and drives the kind of buying behavior you want. The cornerstone of this strategy is knowing where and how to add value.

The right array of employee, customer and brand equity sensors, when cross referenced, will provide a wealth of data for strategic business planning. This will tell you specifically what to do more and less of, while highlighting those actions, features, offerings or strategies which provide the greatest leverage with customers. There is no way to over estimate the importance of this information. It holds the key to quality improvement.

5. MAKING THE MOST OF BRAND EQUITY

Brand management is not as sexy a topic as it was a decade ago, but it is likely to make a comeback in the next few years. Early in the 1990s, recession and deflation put pressure on overpriced brands, taking away some of their panache, along with their fat margins. Well educated customers insisted on knowing what additional value premium brands brought to the party. Those not able to provide a convincing answer found customers shifting to no-name brands.

It is likely premium brands (at least those which learned from their mistakes) are going to make a comeback as the global economy recovers and expands. Underpinning the global expansion will be a focus on value as a by-product of quality over price. However, within this formula, we can expect a subtle but important shift in emphasis *away* from price and *toward* quality. As global growth absorbs excess capacity, power will shift ever so slightly back in favor of quality in the customer's mind.

Although the consumer will remain very much in control and will not allow price gouging, buying decisions will be subtly influenced by perceived quality. A shift of a few degrees in the value equation, one way or the other, can make an enormous difference. After all, markets are made at the margin. The difference between a buyer's and seller's market can be as little as a few percentage points either way.

Renewed Emphasis on Growth

This subtle but important shift back toward quality will be accompanied by increased emphasis on growth as a vital business strategy. Having spent a decade restructuring and cost cutting, many corporations are ready to again focus on customer service, quality and growth. While market leaders would argue they never lost interest in these subjects, evidence shows that much of the corporate world has been absorbed with cost related issues the last few years.

Corporations will also have learned the hard way that once prices are reduced, the market does not allow you to raise them again quickly. A drop of 5% in price can have a huge impact on the bottom line. In fact, in many industries a 5% drop in price, without accompanying cost reduction, can cut profits anywhere from 20-50%.

As growth once more becomes the focus of corporate strategy, brand power will loom large, and for good reason. In a global economy, strong brands have tremendous reach. Like information and capital, premium brands reach across borders. They constitute a sort of global language of their own. The brand equity in Coca-Cola, Nike, Compaq or American Express is not confined to any single country. A consumer buying these products or services in New Delhi, Singapore or New York understands what they are buying. These common expectations are based on an unstated promise communicated without words being spoken.

Another reason premium brands grow in importance is because they are perceived to provide quality, and people are willing to pay a premium for them. Those with strong market positions invariably are perceived as being high quality providers of goods and services by their customers. Firms such as Dupont, Intel, Corning, American Express, 3M, Disney, UPS, Toyota, Sony, Mercedes Benz, Caterpillar, AT&T, Motorola, British Airways, Xerox, and Hewlett-Packard have established market leadership based on perceived quality. If questioned, these companies will, without exception, point to quality management as a key ingredient in both their brand and business success.

Brands with superior perceived quality earn net margins that are nearly four times as high as those perceived to be inferior. The work of author Bradley Gale reveals that quality is a more important driver of competitive position and business results than any other single factor tracked, including market share, cost and total growth of the market.

The PIMS database, one of the largest of its kind anywhere, has shown that over a 20-year period, perceived quality is the best indicator of business success. Even firms with commanding marketshare at the beginning of the period showed steady erosion if perceived quality did not improve. Conversely, those with high perceived quality but low share, saw their market share increase.

Not surprisingly, firms with higher relative perceived quality command larger market share. Thus, they are able to charge a higher price while having costs that are generally lower than most of their competitors. Brands which are established market leaders because of perceived quality can also afford to spend more on advertising. They are under less pressure to offer special promotions and price discounts. The tilt back toward quality will work in favor of these premium brands, at least those which are properly managed.

However, even brands with a commanding market share cannot raise their relative prices beyond a given threshold without convincing customers they are also expanding the quality of their offering. That is why leading brands tend to lose share if they are not quality leaders as well. This loss of share happens even when the affected firms do not raise their relative prices.

In short, if one raises prices without also increasing relative perceived quality, the overall value equation goes into decline. At this point, market share can erode dramatically.

Both premium brands and no-name brands must provide value in order to survive. The difference between the two is that premium brands are under less pressure to reduce price in order to meet the customer's value re-

117

quirements. They avoid this price trap by growing the perceived quality of their offerings as a means of offsetting a somewhat higher price. No-name brands, on the other hand, having relatively low perceived quality, must close the gap by reducing price in the form of promotions, discounts or everyday low pricing. Given a choice, which game would you rather play?

Avoid Being Trapped by Success

Using forcing mechanisms, stressing quality, making continuous improvements, taking advantage of brand equity, and perhaps most of all, managing the customer as an asset are all tried-and-true tools for helping you keep up with shifting value. The task of guarding against the dominance of the *business* by the *organization* is endless, and one from which mature firms must never shirk or tire of.

Having been successful for so long, it is easy for those inside the organization to think their success is the result of their structure and culture. They begin to believe their own press. They forget that all success ultimately comes from adding value for customers.

The internal apparatus, while important, plays only a supporting role in success. It is the customer, not the organization, who is the star of the show and who makes the company successful. In the best of cases, the company and the customer are knit together with trust, common purpose, and shared vision and values.

No problem can be solved within the same consciousness which caused it.
                              —Albert Einstein

Chapter 8

LEARNING DRIVES THE QUEST FOR VALUE

Nothing is more difficult than trying to teach smart people to learn. Market leaders have a particularly difficult time learning because they have been successful based on what they know and *knowing* always interferes with *learning*. However, in times of value decline, what you know can get in the way of what you need to learn.

In an economy increasingly driven by knowledge, learning has become a prerequisite to growth. Not only must people continually learn, but so must organizations. Companies and organizations which learn quickly are able to add value quickly and stay ahead, or at least abreast of, the movement of value. Those unable to learn quickly will fall behind.

So, the age of the learning organization is here. But what *is* a learning organization? It is one which readily absorbs information from its environment, such as market conditions, shifting consumer tastes, rising customer expectations, new competitive threats, regulatory trends, technological shifts, and changes in distribution channels. It then digests and uses it to create new sources of value. In doing so, it creates yet more information which it sends back into the environment—via internal memos, articles, books, case studies, and other means—thus, further contributing to society.

We sometimes confuse the learning organization with the "perfect" organization. Learning organizations are not perfect—they do not do everything right, but they do learn from their mistakes. When something does not work, they correct the error quickly.

When American Express, for example, fumbled its first revolving credit product, the Optima Card, it went back to the drawing board and started again from scratch. When Ford first launched the Taurus and had quality problems with the hoods of the cars, it rejected these inferior components and went to work with suppliers to fix the problem. (In the old days, it would have just repainted the hoods and shipped the product anyway!) Similarly, when a friend of ours bought a Toyota Previa van that turned out to be a lemon, not only did Toyota provide a new one, it took the old one back to the factory in order to reverse engineer the van and find out what had gone wrong.

The big difference between learning and non-learning organizations is in their capacity to respond to errors. Persistence in error is a sure sign of an organization which, in today's diversity parlance, is "learning challenged." That is why people are so infuriated with government these days. It refuses to stop doing things which clearly do not work.

Do not be fooled. Dumb organizations are not necessarily staffed by dumb people. In fact, there may be a lot of very smart people in a dumb organization. They are trapped there by a brain dead organizational apparatus and are often very frustrated. The learning disability usually lies at the organizational level, not with the individual.

For instance, Mikhail Gorbachev, one of the great world figures in the second half of the 20th century, was a smart man trapped in a dumb system. The Soviet bureaucracy was incapable of learning or adapting. Gorbachev recognized that unless the system was reformed, it was doomed. His answer: "*perestroika*," opening the Soviet system to new information.

It was a brilliant, daring gamble, yet it did not work. In the end, the old order could not be saved. The new information brought on by *perestroika* quickly overwhelmed the slow moving, inflexible Soviet system. In his attempt to save the old order, Gorbachev made way for the new. He and Eduard Shevardnadze made history by freeing Eastern Europe, ending the Cold War, and bringing democracy to the Russian people.

CHARACTERISTICS OF A LEARNING ORGANIZATION

1. It Possesses a Learning Ethic

All learning organizations share a learning ethic. They want to learn, and they enjoy it. If something does not work, they are obsessed with finding out why, so they can fix it. Strategic information is an exciting asset to be shared and nurtured. Individuals are encouraged to improve themselves, enhance their skills, and learn as much as they can.

What creates learning organizations? We know that leadership, supporting values, and trust all play a role, as well as incentives. The best incentive for learning is competition. A recent Canadian Conference Board study of innovation discovered that new technologies and methodologies were most likely to be employed by industries facing intense competition. Protected industries or those facing little competition showed no interest or enthusiasm for innovation. They had little incentive to learn, so they did not. All their energy went into finding ways to raise prices without adding value.

2. It Pays Attention

Remember your third grade teacher admonishing you to "pay attention?" Well, she was right. We must be alert to what is going on around us. Information is the primary propellant of renewal. So, successful organizations take in as much information as they can get.

What kinds of information? *All* kinds—happenings in the field, sales promotions which work or do not, suppliers' recommendations, uses for new technology, competitors' ideas, perceptions by satisfied customers, perceptions by unsatisfied customers, what "renegades" on the firm's periphery are thinking, feelings of rank-and-file employees. The list is endless.

In a world transitioning from one economic era to another, the capacity to pay attention to what is happening around you is a prerequisite to survival. Only by taking in and synthesizing information can an organization hope to adapt to fast changing circumstances.

Organizations that cannot absorb information quickly are certain to fall behind. In some industries, the definition of value is shifting so quickly that the penalty for failing to pay attention is almost immediate. The wake up call comes in the form of lost market share or declining margins.

In TAURUS, THE CAR THAT SAVED FORD, author Eric Taub described how in the late 70s and early 80s, Ford designers were cut off from much of the information they needed to redesign cars for a new era. Isolated behind locked doors and armed guards, Ford's designers were working to perfect the soft, mushy "boulevard" ride which insulated the driver from the driving environment—even though customer requirements were moving in entirely the opposite direction.

Ford's market research teams returning from California could literally see foreign cars taking over the road. Foreign car ownership already was over 25% in many California cities and would grow to 40% by decade's end. Consumers opting for Mercedes, BMWs, and Mazda RX-7s were clearly looking for something more than the Crown Victoria had to offer. Numerous studies were done on what this new breed of driver was seeking. Unfortunately, little of this information reached the hermetically-sealed environment of the Ford design labs.

How does an organization pay attention to what is happening in its environment? By actively listening and seeking out new sources of information. These sources can include market research, brand equity analysis, customer satisfaction surveys, focus groups, employee satisfaction surveys, benchmarking data, quality-improvement team data, and interviews with salespeople and front line employees. Information can also come from alliances, mergers, or the hiring of professionals who bring to the organization varying experiences. The key is to systematically seek out this information and inject it regularly into the organization.

The process cannot be left to chance. Obtaining customer and employee's views, brand analysis, market trends, and benchmarking data, for example, must be disciplined and regular. Yet surprisingly few organizations collect such data on a regular basis.

But collecting data by itself is not enough. It must be transmitted throughout the organization loudly enough to be heard and to force change where needed. There is no point having just one sector of the organization undergoing important learning if the rest of the organization is denied access to this information.

For example, field people—those closest to the customer—usually see competitors' moves first or sense a change in customers' preferences. Too often, they cannot get the attention of higher-ups. For data to really have an effect, it must be noticed, then translated into operational objectives, with consequences spelled out.

Vital information, as we have seen, can come from any number of sources. The key is knowing what to do with it. Doomed institutions are often awash in data regarding the need to change. Pan Am, Eastern Airlines, and Wang had plenty of data telling them they needed to do things differently; so did Sears, GM, and IBM. It is not lack of data, but rather the propensity to ignore it, which determines an organization's fate.

3. It's Led by the Enlightened

In the old industrial model, the leader's role was primarily to exercise control. In an economy now driven increasingly by information, the leader's role has changed. Successful leaders must now focus on building organizations which can take in and create new information.

Today's post-modern leaders intuitively know there is a danger in the comfort zone. Very often, a dose of discomforting information is just what is needed to get the organization focused and moving. If the uncomfortable information is fed back to the organization repeatedly and in such a way that it cannot be ignored, it will force the organization off center. This will cause it to oscillate, slowly at first but eventually in wider and wider sweeps away from the status quo. With destabilization, the learning process begins.

If you think about it, this is precisely what occurs when an organization undergoes a crisis. Lost market share, layoffs, mergers, or the prospect of outright closure all cause the organization to veer wildly away from the status quo. People become unnerved, morale drops, irrational behavior occurs, and the organization may even appear at times in danger of becoming dysfunctional. A leader's first instinct in a crisis may be to stabilize the situation, slow the oscillation, and generally "put a lid on it." However, there are times when that is the very worst thing to do.

One client of ours, for example, wanted to know how well it was tracking and delivering its products. What it found was shocking. The firm was mishandling 20% of its deliveries and was completely outperformed by its main competitor.

At first, this benchmarking data was denied and rejected. The CEO kept forcing it back into the system by setting performance goals based on the data. Reluctantly, the company took up the challenge. It set out to reduce shipping errors by 98%. This audacious improvement target could only be achieved by overhauling the entire shipping process. So the company contracted with an integrated logistics firm to reengineer its shipping process, using the latest bar-coding technology. The reengineered process was so successful it became an industry benchmark.

The detonator of this change clearly was the introduction of new information—the data which showed the firm to be bungling 20% of its deliveries. The information would not have been acted upon if the CEO had not forced the data into the system by tying it to compensation and management objectives. Setting the goal of 98% improvement forced the organization out of its comfort zone. As it moved up the learning curve with its new bar-coding and shipping system, the organization acquired a new and powerful core competency in the expedited delivery of products. Ultimately, this was shared in the industry, setting off a new round of learning. Everyone benefited.

Thus, in cases where significant change is needed, it may be in everyone's best interest to keep the organization off balance. In this game of brinkmanship, the key is to bring the organization right to the edge without pushing it over. For instance, when Motorola set its first 10-times-improvement goal, no one believed it was possible to achieve. The reasons given for why it could not be done were legion. At the root of this resistance was the implicit recognition that even *aiming* for such a target would be destabilizing. And achieving it would be traumatic. If Galvin and Fisher, the leaders of the organization, had blinked at that moment, Motorola's quality improvement process would have instantly stalled. Instead, they made it clear that the goal was non-negotiable. In the end, it was the organization which blinked, not its leaders. It is good it turned out that way, the "10 times crisis" set Motorola on the road to world class quality performance and industry leadership.

Another valuable function of a leader is to protect internal sources of information from bureaucratic assault, but he or she must also inject this information into the larger organization. While pockets of new information must be protected, they cannot be so completely cut off that there is no cross-fertilization. This balance can be achieved, for example, by coupling teams from larger and smaller systems, or assigning one or two key individuals from the larger system to act as partners on teams grappling with new concepts. A third is to arrange for a long integration period overseen by a special liaison. In any case, the wise leader manages sources of internal information as valuable assets in the same way one would manage valuable external information.

One of the things which separate human beings from animals and machines is our capacity for introspection. We can look inward and ask ourselves *why*. We are even capable of grappling with paradox, although not always gracefully. "*StarTrek*" fans will recall that troublesome computers in the show's script were made to self-destruct with little more than a command: "Prove that your prime directive is not your prime directive." In trying to ponder the imponderable, the computer implodes.

Not so with mankind—we are at our best when probing beyond our realm of certainty. The challenge for today's leader is to create organizations which more resemble human beings than machines. We must develop organizations capable of introspection—able to take in information, synthesize and create new information. In other words, organizations capable of managing paradox. Such organizations learn daily, and thus they adapt, evolve and thrive.

What Makes an Organization Learning-Disabled?

Conversely, organizations which cannot learn are learning-disabled. How do you identify them? Well, first of all, when they make mistakes, they keep on doing them, no matter how awful the results. In THE MARCH OF FOLLY, Barbara Tuchman cites Philip II, the 16th century monarch of Spain, as a classic example of a slow learner. Even after the disaster of the Armada, in which he lost his whole fleet and nearly bankrupted the country, Philip remained convinced of the "absolute excellence" of his policies.

In World War I, thick headed generals on both sides insisted on employing frontal assaults with massed infantry against entrenched machine guns. Persisting in using 19th century tactics against 20th century weapons, they sent a whole generation of Europe's youth to their deaths. After four bloody years, casualties numbered in the millions!

In more recent history, North American car manufacturers suffered the same problem in the 1970s. Study after study indicated the desire of consumers for higher quality, more fuel efficient automobiles. Yet the car makers simply refused to hear the message. They changed their advertising, altered logos and jingles, added hood ornaments, installed velour seats and fake wood dashboards—anything but do what customers wanted. Not only were they resistant to change, they did not even want to hear about it.

The auto makers were downright hostile to information which pointed to their deficiencies. Quality guru Edwards Deming was not welcomed in Detroit for nearly 20 years. J.D. Powers, who instituted annual comparative quality assessments of automobiles, was once booed from the stage by a combined audience of United Auto Workers leaders and Big Three management. It was not until the 1980s that these companies engaged in the kind of serious Total Quality Management effort necessary to win back their customers.

No Incoming Data

Another characteristic of slow learning organizations is that there is usually little or no external data coming into the organization regarding customers, competition, market conditions, technological trends, or anything else. It is hard to learn when there is nothing to learn with.

Occasionally a dumb organization will find itself with access to good sources of external data, but this information is rarely fed back to the organization in a systematic way. It just goes into a void. Learning-disabled organizations consistently underexploit the information they have. They sometimes even suppress sources of new information. Internal information, such as that which comes from salespeople, technical service reps, and customer service operators, is rarely exploited.

In the 1970s, GM entered the NUMMI (New United Motor Manufacturing, Inc.) joint venture with Toyota to produce a new generation of small cars in Fremont, California. The purpose of the joint venture was to discover the "secret formula" behind the success of Japan's car manufacturer. General Motors selected some of its best and brightest engineers and managers for the NUMMI project.

Within a few years, NUMMI saw amazing gains in quality and productivity as it produced a superb line of new small cars under the Nova brand name. While designing and building the Nova, the GM staff assigned to the project learned there was no "secret" to producing high quality small cars—it was just a question of getting the basics right. These GM staffers were now seed carriers of what Edwards Deming would call "profound knowledge."

126

So what did GM do with this profound knowledge? The company buried it and its "carriers," as deep and far away as it could. The NUMMI graduates were treated as pariahs. No one inside GM wanted anything to do with them. Why? Because their knowledge represented a mortal threat to the status quo at General Motors. It was only years later, with the building of the new Saturn division, that GM cycled back to exploit this insider knowledge.

Paradigm Paralysis

Why do organizations choose to perish rather than take in and respond to new information? Largely because, in effect, the central nervous system of the institution had been damaged. This loss of capacity to absorb information occurs over time and is usually caused by an overabundance of wealth. Cushioned by success, layers of hierarchy build up throughout the organization. To preserve the status quo, these layers invariably block or attenuate market signals.

Sometimes organizations even structure themselves to be dumb and to stay dumb. They set up barriers and buffers to the flow of new data. Early on, for example, it is not unusual for sales personnel to feel a shift in customer requirements, but often they do not have a means of communicating this to the people designing the product.

In a highly fragmented organization, information easily becomes trapped in narrow, functional "silos" or disparate regional units. In this way, vital data can be bottled up at lower levels or among certain groups but cannot be shared with those who need it. For instance, market research, sales, or customer service staffers often have access to mountains of invaluable data which never leaves their department, thus not getting into the hands of decision makers.

Sometimes bureaucracies armed with rules and regulations are structured precisely to keep organizations from learning. Picture this—a real life organization of several thousand people processing hundreds of millions of dollars a year in transactions, isolates itself from the outside world by taking in no external market data. It is flying blind—and *likes it that way*. The many layers of management filter signals moving up the organization. As the signal passes through each layer, it weakens. What little gets to the top is carefully screened, controlled and sanitized.

It is no accident that since the time of Caesar, generals have insisted that front-line reconnaissance units report *directly to them*. This structure is rooted in several thousand years of bitter experience. No sanitation or attenuation of data is permitted. No intermediate layers of command are allowed to get into the way of the truth. How many business executives have similar access to raw, uncontaminated market data? How many know what is *really* going on out there?

To prevent data moving horizontally across the organization, thick "membranes" develop between the vertical silos. Marketing does not talk to Sales, and neither would think of communicating to Design or Manufacturing. In such environments, it is not unusual to find outdated information technology and primitive information support systems; e-mail and networking systems are often regarded as unnecessary fluff. No one communicates with anyone else, and that is the way everyone likes it.

Surely, you may say, such organizations do not exist in this day and age. You *bet* they do! Government is full of them, and the private sector certainly has its share. These organizations erect structures which trap information and blunt opportunity.

Take the case of one financial services firm presented with an immense global marketing opportunity involving a joint venture with a large medical association. However, the firm was organized along regional and product lines while the opportunity spanned the globe and transcended any individual product. As a result, the company had difficulty forming a team to champion the venture.

The client repeatedly found itself dealing with regional or product line executives whose interests and focus were narrower than the new idea. The client wanted to talk about global opportunities, but the firm's executives were only interested in how this impacted "Canada" or "Mexico," or how it affected a particular product line.

The marketing executives who had stumbled across this opportunity in the first place could see that the medical association was becoming impatient, but the marketers had no place to take their pleas for help. There was no person or group within the company responsible for pursuing global opportunities or trans-product lines. In the end, not surprisingly, the medical association took the opportunity to a competitor better organized to meet its global needs.

The kind of self-destructive behavior shown by that firm is almost always rooted in past success. People cling to today's failed paradigm precisely because it was yesterday's successful innovation. Whatever the cause, the result is paradigm paralysis. The organization stops learning.

Sometimes organizations are so busy being successful, they do not have time to learn. And because they are so successful, they can afford to be dumb...for a while. In the course of our work, we have seen organizations which, because they are in the right place, at the right time, catch a value "wave" which carries them to success, despite their best efforts to prevent it. Soon, though, this success becomes a burden because it provides an excuse for not learning.

Organizations unable to learn are unable to adapt and, as a result, perish. This culling process goes on all the time in free market economies—companies falter or even go bankrupt while new ones are born. The morbidity rate increases exponentially during times of economic transition. This is precisely what is happening today, as the rate of turnover in the Fortune 500 increases with each passing year.

Resisting Information

Resistance to new information is not a phenomenon restricted to large, unhealthy organizations, although it is more pronounced in them. Even healthy organizations can resist new information. Why? Because information on rising customer expectations, or a competitor's superior performance, or erosion of brand equity is almost always painful and disruptive. Even information generally known or suspected by insiders can be disruptive, when given tangible form.

That is why consultants often are useful. They feed back information that already exists inside the organization. It is illustrative of the problem that organizations must go outside to learn what they already know. They do so because their internal culture and systems prevent them from hearing the message unless it is packaged and transmitted from outside.

But outsiders cannot force an organization to change, and the mere fact of calling in external help does not guarantee a willingness to change. A firm we know regularly calls in consultants, at considerable expense, to help shift the organizational culture toward greater customer focus. What follows is a predictable and elaborate step dance, in which the external consultant is slowly enculturated and captured by the "middle" of the organization, whose unconscious role is to protect the status quo. The first step in this process calls for the external change agents to be surrounded and bombarded with busy work. The list of activities to be performed grows and grows, as the pace increases. Targets set for years, must now be accomplished in a quarter or a month. Everybody is so busy "doing" things, there is no possibility of learning. Energy displaces reflection, activity crowds out results. The outsiders are soon run off their feet and then the whispering begins in the hallways. "These guys aren't that good...why are we paying so much, we can do this ourselves." Access to the executive floor becomes harder and harder to get. Soon it becomes clear, this latest set of outsiders are on their way out. The organization has once again dodged the bullet. The need to change has been obviated, everything goes back to normal. Pockets of people within the organization may recognize the need for change, but this "prescient few" now duck for cover. This change effort is now over, until the next unsuspecting set of outside consultants are brought in to begin the dance again.

All organizations seek homeostasis, an equilibrium in which everything is predictable. Information, especially discordant information, challenges the status quo and makes homeostasis impossible to achieve. This is precisely why it is resisted. Ironically, what organizations most seek, stability and predictability, usually signal the beginning of death. Organizations too comfortable with the status quo are almost always headed for trouble.

How to Escape Entropy

How does an organization escape this bureaucratic trap and keep itself open to information?

1. *Put Correct Systems in Place*.

As we have mentioned before, the first thing to do is ensure processes are in place for gathering information such as customer satisfaction, employee satisfaction, market research, benchmarking, and brand analysis. Quality and process improvement teams are also excellent sources of new information. In fact, it can be argued that where quality improvement processes have been most successful, it is because they generated vital new information for the organization to synthesize and act upon.

2. Protect Insider Information

When sources of new information come from inside the organization, through alliances, specialty teams, reengineering teams, or quality improvement teams, these sources must be protected from the larger bureaucratic amoeba. Just as external information can be ignored, internal information can be suppressed. This suppression takes many forms, the most effective of which are subtle.

For example, the agents of change are often broken up to better "integrate" them into the larger organization, or they are drawn into a mass of "coordinating meetings." Sometimes suppression takes the form of limiting resources to the new entity or smothering it in bureaucratic busywork. It is hard to engineer a revolution when most of your waking hours are absorbed in trying to understand and complete a host of forms.

It is also a mistake to allow rigid norms, procedures and instructions to be imposed on a team whose aim is to create new information. In life, it is information (DNA) which gives shape to living entities, not the other way around. So it should be in organizations. New information may dictate entirely new structures, organizations and procedures. To allow form to dominate knowledge is a travesty of logic, and it guarantees the triumph of sloth and bureaucracy.

3. Instill Trust and Knowledge-Driven Value

Companies are complex mechanisms with moving parts. They are increasingly information driven and dependent on the expertise of knowledge workers. This combination of complexity, information and value-added knowledge does not lend itself to the old command-and-control environment. These new organizations cannot be "ordered" to perform. They succeed only by virtue of their common purpose and cohesion.

In the new economy, wealth comes from taking in knowledge and synthesizing it, and then creating new value-added knowledge with it. Trust, teamwork and cohesion are essential to this process. This commercialization of knowledge requires sharing. No one can create knowledge-driven value alone in today's work environment. It must be a collaborative effort, but how can there be collaboration without trust?

Today's organizations are increasingly disparate and virtual. Loose knit groups of knowledge workers, networked together electronically, must have a high degree of trust and common purpose in order to perform. In fact, such trust may be all that holds them together. We will take an in-depth look at that in the next chapter.

Use what words you will, you can never say anything but what you are.
                                        —*Ralph Waldo Emerson*

Chapter 9

SOMETHING GAINED...SOMETHING LOST

The great English land owners of the 18th century decided they could make more money by replacing farmers with sheep. Historians now view the great land clearances of that period as inevitable because the economics of the old order simply no longer added up. Nevertheless, it was a sad sight the day highland chieftains turned their own kinsmen out of their homes and sent them packing to Nova Scotia just to make room for animals.

Today, our largest corporations have begun the modern equivalent of the "great clearances." Suddenly, loyalty and corporate affiliation does not count for much; nor do old, obsolete skills. Today, the same sad drama is being played out at IBM, Mobil, Xerox, BellSouth, and other large corporations. These changes, too, are inevitable, but as the whole economy becomes increasingly absorbed in reducing costs and displacing labor, a note of caution is in order. What if, in our lunge to reduce costs, we destroy our capacity to produce wealth? In a number of cases, as we will show, this is precisely what has happened.

A main theme of this book has been that, given today's new value requirements, change is necessary, even desirable. But we must be careful in undertaking this change; otherwise, we risk creating a wasteland—an empty, purposeless, and joyless work environment. Organizations operating in such an atmosphere become brittle and break at the first sign of stress.

Indeed, many corporations have damaged the very systems they set out to improve. The modern firm is a delicate machine made up of work process, technology and people. You can not drop the equivalent of a neutron bomb on the human infrastructure of an organization and expect the machine to go on functioning smoothly.

Painful and Protracted Process

The highland chieftains, too, were richer after the clearances but something irreplaceable had been lost. The system of clan loyalty, which had stood for two millennia or more, was gone forever. The relationship between the chieftain and his followers had become purely economic.

Something is gained and lost in every change. Today, America is in the process of losing its old, Second Wave economy. Although it will gain much in return, the process is proving painful and protracted. Any other society would have already reacted to the level of disruption now being visited upon the U.S. economy. No society anywhere, except perhaps the nations of the Pacific Rim and Eastern Europe, have undergone such dramatic changes within the last 15 years. And there is more to come.

Wise leadership will be required if we are to avoid a reaction to the bloodletting of recent years. Rather than viewing employees as a liability to get rid of, perhaps it is time we concentrated more attention on their value as an asset. Instead of cutting our way to success, we should be focusing on creating wealth and adding value. Instead of shrinking companies, maybe we should be thinking about growing them again.

We might even try to reassure employees that they are still needed and have important work to do. However, that is not the message we are sending when business magazine photos show Mike Hammer, the original reengineering guru, standing on the shores of Lake Ontario brandishing a crowbar over his head. Workers are painfully aware that their bosses are eagerly lining up to attend Hammer's reengineering seminars.

The dilemma confronting today's leaders is that Hammer is half-right. Significant change in our corporate structures and business designs is clearly needed. The economy has changed and so must business. If we do nothing, we will fall behind, our competitive position will deteriorate, productivity will decline, and living standards will drop. So ignoring the problem is not an answer. As Shakespeare reminds us, "Nothing comes from doing nothing."

However, if we must act, we should do so with skill and vision. This is not a sentimental wish but a pragmatic assessment. If we do not

134

learn to better manage today's historic transition, the process could well backfire.

The downtrodden crofters forced off their land in the 18th century had little recourse and few options. The New World offered their only way out and served as a social safety valve. Had this option not existed, violence would almost certainly have followed. Today's displaced workers do have options. In a democracy, there is always recourse to the ballot box. If the critical mass of voting citizens decide events are moving too fast, they will simply slow them down politically. As in the 1930s, people could again begin to blame the "market mechanism" itself for their troubles.

An Underlying Moral Question

Beneath the trauma lies an underlying moral question regarding the very purpose of business and markets. *Why do they exist?* Is it to make profits, create wealth, serve shareholders, or create jobs for employees? The answer is: all of these and more. Corporations exist to serve the interests of shareholders, employees and customers. However, they should exist to also serve the interests of society, to make life better. If firms perform well, they are rewarded with profits. Business should be an instrument of social progress, with profits, dividends, salaries and rising share values as by-products of meeting this larger requirement.

By adding value, corporations serve society. In the course of adding value, the best interests of all stakeholders are also served—so long as these interests are kept in balance. But any time the balance of interest between shareholders, customers and employees swings too far in one direction or the other, value suffers and so does society.

For instance, in the late 1970s and 1980s shareholders perceived that some management teams were putting their own interests ahead of owners. This brought on a wave of shareholder revolts, corporate raiding, leveraged buyouts, and a renewed focus on corporate governance. Or, take the auto industry in the 1950s, 60s and 70s. While prices went up, quality went down as it was arrogantly assumed in Detroit that no one would mind or even notice being fleeced. The United Auto Workers and management of the Big Three met regularly to carve up the pie and yell at one another. Completely self-absorbed, they lost sight of the customer. Then

135

one day, they looked up and found their customers were gone—they had moved on in search of better quality and service.

Losing customers is a sobering experience and it shocked the auto industry out of its complacency. That was the beginning of the U.S. auto recovery. From that moment of awakening, it took Detroit more than a decade to catch up with its customers. Recovering was hard, tough work. Had the industry been afforded the protection from competition which it sought, it would almost certainly have faltered long before the course was run. The auto industry learned to add value again only because it was forced to; this recovery was driven by pain, not virtue.

Now our society is again grappling with whether corporate America is being wise. It is a matter of perception. Just look at the organizations which have each laid off tens of thousands of employees since 1992: IBM, 122,000; AT&T, 83,000; GM, 74,000; U.S. Postal Service, 55,000; Sears, 50,000; Boeing, 31,000; Hughes Aircraft, 25,000; McDonnell-Douglas, 21,000; BellSouth, 21,000; Digital Equipment, 20,000.

Will those layoffs result in long-term improvements?
In some cases, yes. We are starting to learn that not all layoffs improve value for shareholders or society. Dominance by any one stakeholder group usually results in a loss of focus on value, the true purpose of commerce. Is the balance out of whack today? Perhaps, but we are too close to these events to say for sure. A decade from now, historians will be better able to pass judgment.

However, what is clear is that employees in large corporations are being pulled through a keyhole. In the rush to chase value and to restructure, employees have suddenly become expendable and are no longer "our greatest asset," as firms used to boast. Now they have become "our greatest liability," or at least that is the message we are sending to them.

Re-engineers Run Amok

During the reengineering craze of the 1990s, we smashed hierarchies, dismantled work processes, shredded relationships, shattered confidence, denigrated old loyalties, and turned middle managers into an endangered species. In short, we put the American economy through a meat grinder and buried forever the 20th century concept of corporate loyalty.

Large corporations have been restructuring and laying off workers at unprecedented rates for a decade now. This wave of restructuring has moved beyond manufacturing into services and will soon be impacting the public sector. No one is immune.

At first, restructuring was prompted by offshore competition which forced American manufacturers to get serious about quality and productivity. Later, in the early 1990s, downsizing was driven by global deflationary pressure. The end of the Cold War also had an impact as it rendered huge chunks of our military industrial complex redundant.

The root cause of all of this restructuring is the emergence of a global information-driven, knowledge-driven economy. This is forcing the overhaul of our old Second Wave economic structures. The forces behind this transition are immensely powerful, and the adjustments required are large and painful.

In 1990, 316,000 jobs were eliminated with the figure increasing to 555,000 jobs in 1991. In 1993, the figure was again at the half-million mark and by 1994, it was 516,000. Job losses in 1995 are again expected to top half a million. Although more new jobs are being created than are being lost, this is cold comfort to those displaced in this process.

Focus on Closings

By amplifying the downsizing phenomenon, the press makes things worse. After all, bad news is "news." The closing of a plant or the reduction of a workforce is the sort of dramatic stuff which lends itself to catchy headlines. On the other hand, the wealth creation process is subtle and less visible. While local newspapers and TV newscasts focus on plant closings, they fail to see the opening or expansion of a business across the street; it is invisible to them. Why? Because one is "news" and the other is not. This might explain why as things got better in the 1980s, the headlines got worse.

Not surprisingly, employees buffeted and bruised by these changes feel bitter and helpless. As one Xerox employee put it, "Five years ago, I felt pretty close to comfortable, but now I feel that I'm part of a big wheel that just keeps rolling. Whatever the wheel wants to do, it's going to do." This feeling of helplessness raises anxiety, stress and disorientation. Those who find themselves unemployed, even temporarily, suffer a blow to their confidence and self-esteem. The unemployed worker loses daily association with fellow workers and is cut off not only from a source of income but also from the social system that surrounds work. The whole process is traumatic.

To make matters worse, many organizations have cut costs and laid off employees without redesigning work processes. They call it "reengineering," but the only thing they have reengineered is their budget. One organization we know responded to recessionary margin pressure with a spasm of cost cutting initiatives. It all made sense on paper, but service levels quickly declined and customer satisfaction plummeted. As a result, when the market came back following the recovery, the firm began to lose share.

Another firm, Northern Telecom, dramatically cut its service and support functions during the early 90s. Then, when it began to experience glitches during the introduction of new products, it did not have the capacity to handle them. The company experienced record losses before restoring its former service and support levels.

Increasingly, questions are being asked about how effective restructuring and reengineering have been. In too many cases, the answers are mixed, profits do not improve, productivity remains low, and shareholder value does not increase. It is now becoming clear that many of the reengineering efforts of the early 1990s were mismanaged. Lacking any clear link to corporate strategy (sometimes reengineering *was* the strategy), these efforts became little more than brutal exercises in reducing costs.

A study by the Wyatt Company of 531 company downsizings found that few of them have produced long term benefits. Only 46% increased earnings, 34% increased productivity, and just a third improved customer service. Another study was even more damning. University of Wisconsin researcher Kenneth De Meuse followed companies for five years, including two years before downsizing and two years after it was completed. Over the five years, the downsized companies showed profit margins of 6%, 6%, 4%, 2% and 0%. Companies which did not downsize showed margins of 6%, 6%, 7%, 6% and 5%.

Urged on by the reengineers, the downsizing that occurred in the first half of the decade had a herd-like quality about it, with many organizations taking an ax to their own wealth creation machinery. H.J. Heinz, for example, began a cost cutting initiative in the early 1990s which included a significant reduction in the workforce. However, quality began to decline as overworked Starkist employees began to leave tons of meat on the fish bones. Ultimately, the firm reached for a quality solution which turned conventional cost cutting theory on its ear: quality could be improved and money made by actually *adding* employees.

At many other firms where restructuring did work and profits improved, employees found they were still subject to layoffs. If hard work and high profits can not protect your job, what *can*? Nor does it help when major corporations cut workers' salaries while making record profits and awarding executives multi-million dollar bonuses. Feeling betrayed and burned out, many employees are withdrawing all emotional commitment from their work. Every morning they get up and just go through the motions. That is hardly a recipe for productivity or quality.

As firms renew their value propositions and jettison under-performing assets and obsolete structures, they are engaging in massive economic renewal. Unfortunately, renewal is often accompanied by layoffs and dislocation. People are inevitably caught in the middle and hurt. Ultimately, most of them take their talents to other sectors of the economy that are growing and in need of their skills. However, the transition is always painful and bloody.

An Inevitable Reaction

We are not arguing against downsizing, which is inevitable as we transition from one economic era to another. However, we do need to keep in mind that downsizing takes place in a societal setting. It occurs because society "allows" it to happen. Such forbearance is based on the implicit assumption that downsizing will improve performance. If that turns out not to be the case, a social reaction of some sort is inevitable.

Luckily, America has a higher tolerance for this sort of disorder than other societies. It was, after all, a nation founded on revolution. We would be foolish to assume this tolerance is infinite. If the business community pursues cost reductions or reengineering goals to the utter disregard of society as a whole, or if it makes a mess of these efforts and produces few results, a reaction of some sort is inevitable. If we are not careful, we could undermine the very trust and confidence which holds the American economic system together.

If you think that is preposterous, remember what happened in the 1930s. The Depression was perceived by many as a failure of the business community. Scapegoating the private sector, citizens turned to government for solutions, and we have been living with the problems of big government ever since.

Could it happen again? Yes, but what form this reaction would take is uncertain. Today, government itself is held in such disrepute that people are unlikely to turn to the public sector for a solution, except as a last resort. As Isaac Newton reminds us, "For every action, there is an equal and opposite reaction."

So, how would this reaction manifest itself? One indicator may be the increasing reluctance of top university graduates to work for large corporations. Generation "X" does not trust big government, but neither does it trust big business. A deadlier sign of discontent is the rise of extremist, anti-immigrant, anti-trade, and anti-big business political constituencies, such as those who opposed NAFTA or supported Pat Buchanan in his run for the presidency. To the right of this movement are even more dangerous elements—radical, nihilist groups who are against all forms of social order or governance. Like the anarchists of the 19th century, they are *against* everything and *for* nothing. With bombings, shootings and violence their trademark, this far right fringe has become an ever greater threat to American society.

Challenge and Response

In summarizing their lifetime study of history, Will and Ariel Durant found that challenge is the chief source of renewal. A challenge successfully met propels society forward. The greater the challenge, the greater the potential "renewal."

When asked what determines if a challenge will be met, they answered: "It depends upon the presence or absence of initiative and of creative individuals with clarity of mind and energy of will..." To these two criteria, we venture to add a third: the *moral conviction* to do what is right. Arguably, we have more need of strong moral leadership today than ever before.

As we pass from one economic era to another, our society is being challenged to redefine itself. In such a period of flux, nothing is guaranteed—not even the free market system. The case for democracy and capitalism must continually be made in the form of actions, not just good intentions.

As citizens and leaders, we must go to great lengths to explain to employees and communities why today's painful changes are necessary and what the ultimate benefits will be. We must take time to explain the big picture to our employees, suppliers and the community. We should not take for granted that everyone understands the forces driving these changes; in fact, most people *do not* They are too busy reacting to these forces to give much thought to their origins.

Redefining Leadership

Explaining "why" will not be enough. Business leaders must also act responsibly in undertaking large-scale restructuring and change, and they must offer leadership suitable for these unsettled times. It may be necessary to redefine the very dimensions of modern leadership. This re-definition is likely to take us back to such basics as courage, honor, forti-tude, and most importantly, leading by example. Leaders involved in large scale change must share not only information, but also hardships and risks with those they lead.

If this sounds a little old-fashioned and idealistic, *so be it*! It works. Nineteen- and 20-year-old corporals understand implicitly why they cannot lead people who do not trust or respect them. Why is this truth so hard to understand for a 50-year-old executive with above average intelligence, a couple of degrees, and years of experience?

The Core of Commerce

Subject to the torque and stress of change, organizations and in-stitutions must hold together or risk being torn apart. Like the wing of an aircraft in turbulence, they must flex without breaking. Webster's diction-ary defines cohesion as "the act or state of uniting or sticking together, the property of unity." The military has done extensive studies on why some units come apart under pressure, while others grow closer and stronger. The one most important factor which emerges from these studies is *trust*. The larger and stronger the radius of trust, the greater the cohesion.

Trust has been at the core of commerce and business since the very first exchange of goods. Without trust, there can be no commerce. Think about it! When you strike a bargain, you trust it will be honored.

When you pay the agreed amount, you "trust" that you will receive the contracted goods or services. The person selling you the product trusts you to pay the agreed amount and trusts that the currency is genuine.

At another level, the seller is trusting that the central bank which issued the currency will redeem it at face value and/or protect its underlying value. If chaos, dishonesty or incompetence undermines this base level of trust, the whole system quickly unravels, as we saw happen in Germany in the 1920s. This explains why inflation has such a pernicious impact on the economy—it undermines "trust" in the currency, one of the pillars supporting commerce.

For a free market system to work, there must be a foundation of trust which underpins the economy. The rules must be clear, the judiciary honest, and corruption minimized. People must believe their money is safe in banks and its value will not depreciate without warning. They must trust the bulk of their suppliers, customers, and employees since no one could possibly hire enough guards and spies to oversee them all. Without trust, the whole wealth-creation process disintegrates.

A Major Competitive Advantage

What is true of the economy in general turns out to be true, too, within organizations. A recent study by a major consumer products firm sought to discover the most important cause of "regretted turnover"—people leaving whom the company had wished to retain. The number one factor was a low trust relationship with their boss. In another study involving many firms, employees were asked what qualities they most valued in leaders, and the most frequent response was "credibility." In a third study, researchers concluded that corporate culture can have a significant impact on a company's bottom line and that a key aspect of performance enhancing cultures is their trustworthiness. These are just three of many directional signs pointing toward trust as a critical factor in organizational success or failure.

When value is pouring into an industry, it is possible to be profitable in almost any corporate culture. Thus, bad habits frequently become imbedded in the culture. When value begins to shift, trust becomes imperative, and most employees do not think their workplace manifests trust. *Industry Week* in a survey a few years ago showed that 87% of the workers polled believe it is "very important" that management be "honest, upright and ethical," but only 39% believed that described their leaders.

Trust, says management author and speaker Gordon Shea, is the "miracle ingredient in organizational life—a lubricant that reduces friction, a bonding agent that glues together disparate parts, a catalyst that facilitates action." Conversely, low trust begets poor results, and poor results can't be tolerated, especially when an organization is chasing value.

Over the long haul, then, trust is a major competitive advantage. To survive and prosper in today and tomorrow's global economy will be difficult, if not impossible, for organizations in which people do not trust one another.

Organizations desperately need ideas, innovation, risk taking, open communication, and collaborative problem solving. Employees, for their part, want to feel cared about and to feel worthwhile because they are making a significant contribution.

Low trust inhibits both goals. Risk taking, innovation and collaboration suffer while suspicion and defensiveness increase and worker energy is diverted into non-productive political behavior. Thus, creativity and resourcefulness are squandered.

What Can Leaders Do?

Lack of trust is ultimately lethal. An organization lacking it is eventually going to be dead in the water. But the good news is that lack of trust can be cured. Trust can be built by an organization by scrupulously underscoring trustworthy policies: telling the truth all the time, keeping agreements, and making sure everyone stays well informed. Individuals also have a large role to play in trust building.

Too many managers, even top managers, when discussing trust in their organization, speak in the language and hopeless tone of victims. They seem to be saying they are powerless to change it. That mindset becomes a self-fulfilling prophecy.

Since the level of trust fluctuates over the history of an organization, *something* causes it. External buffeting has an effect, of course. It is clear that the sum of individual human decisions and action can push trust in either direction. Far from being helpless victims, we can help create our own future.

143

The basic unit of trust in a relationship is between two individuals. The prevailing organizational culture bears upon each such pair. Yet, the reverse is also true: each high trust relationship models the possibility of trust and sends that message back to the culture. If enough individuals set about building a high trust relationship, the culture cannot remain unaffected. Over time, it will absorb the trust and enshrine the behavior which produced it.

Our model of trust is a temple with four pillars: Openness, Honesty, Credibility and Respect, undergirded by the need for Consistency.

Openness means sharing one's thoughts and feelings and being receptive to the same in others. It's self-disclosure as opposed to guardedness. As that openness is reciprocated, the trust level in the relationship is nudged higher.

Honesty, as used here, means giving truthful, complete feedback to others, for better or worse. "Feedback," says Ken Blanchard, co-author of THE ONE-MINUTE MANAGER and other motivational books, "is the breakfast of champions." People want and need to know how they are doing. Employees will trust those who consistently talk to them straight.

Credibility means making and keeping agreements. You do so by (1) making only those agreements you intend to keep, (2) avoid making, or accepting, unclear or fuzzy agreements, (3) give early notice if an agreement must be broken, and (4) if you *must* break an agreement, make sure you initiate the renegotiation and try to mend your chipped credibility.

Respect means honoring five unspoken requests that people make of each other in any relationship. They are:

1. Listen non-judgmentally
2. Acknowledge differences without assigning blame
3. Give credit to others for their unique and special qualities
4. Look for positive intentions
5. Tell others your truth compassionately

If you honor all five unspoken requests, the other person will consistently feel respected, even cared about. When you are able to employ all four pillars—openness, honesty, credibility, and respect—your relationships will tend to be high-trust ones.

When all the employees of an organization follow suit—with sponsorship and role models offered by management—the corporate culture gains the critical competitive advantage of everyone working together to create a successful enterprise. This is a powerful medicine for any organization.

Dialogue Across the Centuries

Executives today must walk a thin moral line when undertaking needed restructuring. They must redesign their business to meet the customer's perception of value. They must also be fair to those hard working employees affected by these changes. Most executives do not set out each morning to wreck people's lives, but they do have hard economic choices to make.

In making these difficult choices, they undertake a moral debate as old as mankind itself. What is the *right* thing to do? Do you wait and hope things improve on their own, or aggressively overhaul your business to better conform to shifting perceptions of value? When you act, whose interests do you protect?

It is our belief that you are on shaky moral ground if you undertake painful and disruptive restructuring or reengineering for the sole purpose of adding short term value for shareholders. On the other hand, to make difficult changes in order to keep an organization healthy and competitive is an argument with moral weight. Certainly it is an argument you can take to employees and the community and expect to receive a fair hearing.

The outcome is the same either way, but the grounds for making the decision are entirely different. One caters to the needs of a single stakeholder group, while the other tries to balance the long-term interest of all parties. The importance of knowing "why" you are undertaking major change is vitally important because it profoundly impacts the implementation. If your only goal is to enrich shareholders, you need not involve other stakeholders in the decision making process or explain to anyone the reasons for your actions; you simply "do it to them" and hope the inevitable resistance can be overcome.

On the other hand, if you believe your decision is in the best long-term interest of the organization, you must involve all stakeholders. You must keep them informed, seek their assistance, do your utmost to support those adversely effected by the change. As the leader of such a change effort, you would have to model your behavior on that of the 19-year-old corporal we discussed earlier. You must provide physical leadership and be present with those impacted and share in their hardships and disappointments. This requires a higher order of leadership than just maneuvering a restructuring plan through the board of directors.

So it all comes down to making an informed moral decision, one you can live with as a human being and sell to all stakeholders. Such decisions are characterized by:

1. A superb communications plan. Do not skimp here.
2. Effective strategies for supporting those affected.
3. A process for involving stakeholders in developing and implementing the plan.
4. Openness and honesty. Do not be afraid to make yourself vulnerable.
5. Explaining the "why" again and again.
6. Sharing the hardship. Be physically present as often as possible.
7. Sending the right signals. Do not pay yourself wads of bonus money, for example, while others must endure pay cuts.
8. Managing the change so as to enhance, not erode, teamwork.
9. Trying to present a hopeful picture of the future.

In our focus on economic drivers, new methodologies, and state-of-the-art technology, it is easy to forget the metaphysical and spiritual side to change. In doing so, we take enormous risks. The lessons of history are clear and compelling: institutions which ignore the human and moral components of change are destined to fail.

New studies indicate that balancing the interests of stakeholders appears to pay off. James Heskett and John Kotter of Harvard studied 32 companies over 11 years to determine the characteristics of high performing cultures. One of their most striking conclusions was that firms which consistently produce superior business results share one fundamental characteristic: the leadership does not let the short-term interest of the shareholders override all other business considerations. Decisions in these firms are made with an eye toward long-term impact. This is not the sort of thinking that lends itself to a crowbar approach to reengineering.

And how can it be otherwise? Can any institution undertake rapid change without first being cohesive? Can we dispense with trust and teamwork in our rush to get the job done? These are simple but profound questions to which most executives would instinctively be sympathetic. If we believe trust is important, why do we do so little to reinforce it in times of change?

Adam Smith, whom many people do not realize was first and foremost a professor of moral philosophy, built his theories on the basis of a moral community. According to Smith, while the market has a way of separating the efficient from the inefficient, it was never meant to be a substitute for moral responsibility. We would do well to reflect on the difference.

Part IV

Big Government's

Value Crisis

Great nations are never impoverished by private, though they are sometimes by public, prodigality and misconduct.

—*Adam Smith*

Chapter 10

WHY THE PUBLIC SECTOR IS HEMORRHAGING VALUE

Government, not only in America, but throughout the world is in crisis. Value is bleeding out at an astonishing rate. Simply put, government—by not reacting quickly enough to the present value crisis—is *flirting with extinction.*

Up to now, we have discussed the movement and transformation of value primarily as an economic phenomenon transforming business. It is impossible to discuss the movement of value without touching on the public sector, which is experiencing the greatest decline of all. Unlike the value problem in business, though, the crisis in government involves more than just issues of strategy and technique.

Government faces a crisis of relevancy which is every bit as serious as the one it faces regarding its performance. Beyond the erosion of value that results from not meeting customers' expectations or by falling behind the information value-added curve, big government today finds itself on the wrong side of powerful economic and historical forces. The shift in power toward a global, knowledge-driven economy and away from the old, national, analog economy is rendering government less relevant each day.

This loss of relevancy is at the root of today's crisis in the public sector. In fact, loss of relevance erodes value faster than either high prices or performance failures. As long as a product or service is relevant, value can always be added.

When something *no longer matters*, value erosion is inevitable. When declining relevance combines with high prices and poor performance, value decline is instant and massive. Propeller driven planes, for ex-

151

ample, have been eclipsed by jets for most long haul commercial use, but they have not totally disappeared. They are still used by private pilots and for short haul transport, and they probably will not ever totally vanish because of their ruggedness and fuel efficiency.

However, they are outdated, and you probably would not want to fly across the Atlantic on one of them today. Further, improving the technical quality of the propeller is not going to bring them back. That type of aircraft has been overtaken by technology. Its value to the industry and to the airplane-riding public has eroded, and thus, its function has been greatly reduced.

That is what is happening with big governments today. They are going the way of prop planes. While governments are still around and can perform important functions, they are clearly becoming less relevant in the eyes of many constituents. This explains why huge portions of the voting population do not bother to vote. There was a time when these nonvoters were largely disenfranchised and poorly educated. Today, the profile of nonvoters is changing. Increasingly, well-educated citizens are casting a vote of no-confidence by dropping out of the electoral process. This is a sure sign of declining relevancy.

To understand why big government is losing relevance and hemorrhaging value, we must go back to the fundamentals of government. Remember, at the center of the nation-state's relevance was national security and control of commerce and trade. Today, war is increasingly a transnational business, as the Gulf War Coalition showed. And control of money is no longer a national prerogative; Alan Greenspan, chairman of the Federal Reserve, has conceded as much.

Thus, in a world riding the power curve into the global, knowledge quadrant, the nation-state and its government apparatus are losing relevance.

REASONS FOR LOSS OF RELEVANCY

1. *Obsolete Systems*. The operating systems and structures of big government are rooted in another era. Its structure, based on large command-and-control bureaucracies, is archaic and incapable of learning or adapting. Today's economy is infinitely more complex than in the 1930s and '40s, when the structural and philosophical foundations of big government were laid.

Back then, people thought of the economy as a great machine. Today, we know it more closely resembles a great ecosystem. Thus, an Information Age economy, like a marsh or tropical rainforest, is too complex to be designed, regulated or controlled by any bureaucracy. To live, the system must evolve spontaneously. Who planned the Amazon rainforest? For that matter, who planned the personal computer or software industries?

2. *Obsolete Theories*. It is also apparent that government's basic operating theories are outdated. The idea that government can engineer a social revolution with tax and fiscal policy is based on flawed theory. It assumes laws will impact society and the economy in the ways intended by its authors. Just the opposite has often proved true.

Well intentioned efforts to eliminate poverty and support the less privileged have produced unexpectedly perverse results. Instead of promoting economic self-sufficiency, some of our support programs encourage dependence, family breakup, and single parenthood. As a result, single parenthood has emerged as the single biggest contributor to rising poverty in America, especially among children.

Similarly, efforts to redistribute wealth, provide health care, and enhance the quality of workers' lives through high payroll taxes has led to a decline in full-time employment and a rise in the number of part-time or free-lance workers who don't have health care or other benefits—again, just the opposite of what was intended.

3. *Big Cost-Small Payoff*. We are not wiser, healthier, safer or happier as a result of 50 years of big government. Nor is society necessarily more just. However, we do pay more. In most developed economies, people now work half the year just to pay off their tax obligations. In the United States, workers' income from January through the first of June belongs to the government and that amount is growing. (If the indirect costs of government—such as tariffs and the cost of regulations—are included, the figure extends to July 1.)

Not surprisingly, according to a recent Harris poll, nearly two-thirds of Americans feel the American Dream has become harder to achieve. Why? They lay the biggest blame on government spending (73%) and high taxes (61%). This represents value erosion on a historic scale.

In jurisdiction after jurisdiction, citizens have begun to resist the state's claim on national wealth. In countries where the government controlled virtually all national assets, their economies have collapsed amid revolution and chaos. In democratic states, the reaction has been more muted, but the tide of resistance and resentment is rising.

4. *Coming Rollback in Transfer Programs.* Big government still retains some relevancy to those who receive money from it. Increasingly, the whole focus of government consists of transferring money from some population groups to others. That game, like a great Ponzi scheme, is about to collapse.

Why? Because that role impedes economic growth and is no longer affordable on today's scale. Governments throughout the developed world are discovering, though belatedly, that there are indeed limits on their ability to tax, borrow and spend. This realization will soon lead to a retreat of the welfare state and a rolling back of entitlement programs. In time, this retreat could become a rout as governments are forced to abandon expensive transfer payments.

As Peter Drucker points out in his book, POST-INDUSTRIAL SOCIETY, "In every single developed country, governments have reached the limits of their ability to tax and their ability to borrow. They have reached these limits during boom times when, according to modern economic theory, they should have built up sizable surpluses. The fiscal state has spent itself into impotence."

Government has mostly failed in its attempts to redistribute wealth. Instead, the overwhelming evidence points to productivity and economic growth as the keys to wealth redistribution. So growth, not government, is the great equalizer.

5. *The Dawn of the Age of Abundance.* Another reason government is losing relevance is that we are moving toward an Age of Abundance made possible by an explosion of knowledge. Ideas, like capital, cannot be contained within the borders of any single nation.

Winning in this Age of Abundance will require governments to think globally and focus increasingly on growth and wealth creation. Those governments and other institutions which fail to transition from managing scarcity to managing abundance will become increasingly irrelevant. They will bleed value and be pushed out of the way, as we will discuss in Chapter 12.

Microcosm of the Crisis

In short, the reasons central governments were created in the first place are going away and with them, so is a portion of government's relevance. As the makers of prop planes learned, it's hard to add value if your product does not matter much any more. To reverse this situation, central governments must redefine their role and reason for being. They must find a new source of relevance. They must ask, "*Why do we exist?*" or even "*Why does society allow us to exist?*"

To see a microcosm of government's crisis of relevancy in a Third Wave economy, just follow the debate in Washington on regulating the Internet. The Beltway has been hungering to get its hands on the Internet since rumors of its existence first reached Capitol Hill. Now, under the guise of protecting our children from smut, legislators propose regulating content on the Net. This, in turn, could lead to the creation of something like a Department of the Internet, staffed with high-tech bureaucrats and cybercops. The next step might be to try to tax the Internet.

Regulating the Internet will not work. The Internet is a classic by-product of the information-driven, global economy. It does not reside in any single country; it is everywhere and it is nowhere. It has no single center of gravity, no real headquarters and its output moves around the world at the speed of light. Attempts by a slow moving, Second Wave institution, such as government, to capture the Internet will prove as futile as capturing quicksilver. In truth, the Internet, like capital and knowledge, has slipped the leash and gone global; and there's little that government can do about it.

Another telling example of globalization was the debate over the now infamous "Clipper Chip," a silicon chip designed for use in voice-encryption systems. It became a focal point in a tug-of-war between the forces of Second Wave national sovereignty and Third Wave global consumer sovereignty.

As more people do business over cordless phones, the need to protect privacy has become increasingly important. Thus, many companies have begun marketing voice encryption systems to ensure private conversations can't be listened to. However, these scramblers also make it more difficult for law-enforcement officials to bug the phones of suspected criminals.

So the U.S. government proposed that all voice encryption systems made in the United States be built around the Clipper Chip, which has a built-in port allowing authorities to decode the conversation. That made sense from the viewpoint of national sovereignty. From the perspective of a Third Wave global economy, it was absurd.

No one with the interest and money to buy a voice encryption system was going to buy one which was "compromised" from the beginning. If the U.S. government forced American manufacturers to use the Clipper Chip, consumers around the world would opt overwhelmingly for French or German equipment. Needless to say, the United States was in no position to force foreign manufacturers to adopt the Clipper Chip.

So the only way the Clipper Chip would work was if it were adopted as a global standard—and that was not about to happen any time soon. Meanwhile, U.S. manufacturers were outraged at the government's threat to cripple them, and the Feds, mystified by all the fuss, eventually backed off.

Another example of how the rules have changed is the issue of regulating derivatives, those arcane financial instruments which have the financial world in such a tizzy these days. Derivatives are sold globally, and no single nation can control them. Congress held hearings but concluded that any attempt to suppress or closely control derivatives would just force the market offshore.

Thus, the problem would not go away, it would just go elsewhere. Skirmishes like this between national sovereignty and global consumer sovereignty will become common in the next few years.

So, What _Is_ the Role of Government?

So does central government have a role to play in a global, information-driven world? Yes, but it is not the role it has played for the past 300 years. If government is to stay in business, it must redefine why it exists and reengineer how it operates.

Government will not disappear overnight; history does not move that quickly. Defense concerns will remain important, central banks will continue to operate, and the State Department will still execute foreign policy, at least for the foreseeable future.

Because the competitive free market system necessarily creates winners and losers, some government probably needs to be around to help those who are thrown out of work, are injured on the job, or otherwise get caught in the gears of capitalism. In that limited sense, government may always be needed to serve as something of a support arm for the private sector. It is also in the domestic arena where the coming changes will become most apparent, as government increasingly shifts its focus from managing scarcity to managing growth.

As the global economy shifts into an abundance cycle, government's primary role will be to change from redistributing wealth to creating wealth by promoting long term growth. Only by doing so can government regain some measure of relevance and reverse the deterioration of value. Luckily, there are models out there of governments which are doing this successfully, but few are found within the clubby environment of the OECD (Organization for Economic Cooperation and Development) where the most developed countries in the world reside. As usual, tomorrow's models are emerging on the periphery, far from the traditional centers of power.

If central government's role changes, so must its basic design. To perform different functions, it must take on different forms and adopt different philosophies. These forms and philosophies are already taking shape in a handful of countries, as we will discuss in the next chapter.

Fifty Years of Big Government

During the past 50 years, governments at all levels have grown and expanded into areas and functions which now encompass almost every aspect of life and society. As we stand at the cusp of the 21st century and examine what this growth in government has wrought, it is clear something is wrong. Government, which is now involved in almost everything, does very little of it well.

Sadly, there is an inherent withering of the spirit in much of government. In the early, heady days of many agencies, an enviable idealism and an entrepreneurial fervor exists, akin to that seen in young companies. The mandate is clear and fresh. Workers are full of zeal, and enthusiasm pervades. Many of big government's finest moments have been in such settings—the early Peace Corps, NASA, Civilian Conservation Corps, and the Works Progress Administration (WPA) where getting the job done took precedence over just getting by. Theirs was an élan, a vigor that was palpable.

Then something happens. Enthusiasm fades and the barnacles of bureaucracy grow. Without the stimulus of competition, without the lure of substantial reward, and without the sword of possible extinction hanging over the heads of all involved, the pace slows and the spirit dims. Soon, the agency loses sight of why it exists—and then it begins acting as if it exists for its own sake. We then get a by-the-numbers performance where we once may have had energized people with ideas.

Can that be changed? Our best thinkers ought to be working on that. They should look, for example, at civil service—another well-intentioned idea that has largely backfired—and how incompetent civil-service employees could be more easily fired. Or whether, under a proposal offered by Charles Peters, editor-in-chief of *The Washington Monthly*, 50% of all government workers should be political appointees. That, Peters says, would give citizens more control by allowing them to toss out the elected officials—and their bureaucrats—if levels of service were perceived as poor.

Another idea worth taking a look at is whether semi-autonomous commissions—along the lines of the recent military-base closing commissions—could help government make some of the tough decisions which pork-barrel politics now prevents. These questions are mounting and require urgent attention.

A Better Referee Than Player

To its credit, government does appear to be reasonably good at setting rules, although, as we will see, it has a natural propensity to set too many. On the positive side, government forced the auto manufacturers, for example, to install air bags and increase fuel efficiency, strictures which actually helped Detroit add value. Without nudging by the government, it is doubtful the auto makers would be now working on the electric car, which promises vast environmental and economic benefits. Government also played an important role in focusing industry on the need to achieve higher quality.

It was government which broke up the AT&T monopoly, thus jump starting competition among telephone, TV, and cable companies and setting us on the road to the information super highway. Government is beginning to deregulate utilities, giving the consumers the right to pick and choose among gas and electric companies the way they now can select among long-distance phone companies. All of this activity is in line with the trend toward transcending narrow political boundaries and putting the consumer in the driver's seat.

So, using a sports analogy, you could say government is pretty decent at keeping score and maintaining a level playing field. If given close scrutiny, then, it may be a good commissioner or referee, but it is clearly a poor player on the field.

Less Than Competent

Government has proved less than competent in most of the things it does beyond its core regulatory, law enforcement, and defense functions. Think about it: from the post office, through Medicare, Medicaid, Social Security, food stamps, education—and on and on—government has turned into a second rate supplier of goods and services. That is not our verdict but the verdict rendered by most of its customers today. Even in its regulatory function, it is often an obstacle to wealth creation rather than a help.

For example, virtually anyone starting a business in the United States must get licenses and permits from a plethora of different agencies. A manager of even a small chemical company is required to have a business license, a permit for hazardous material storage, a permit for an air pressure tank, a permit from the Occupational Safety and Health Administration for a liquefied petroleum gas tank, a compressed gas permit, a hazardous waste permit from the Environmental Protection Agency, and a resale number.

Moreover, the trend is alarming. In REINVENTING GOVERNMENT, Al Gore notes that forest rangers in the 1960s could carry the list of rules in their shirt pockets. Now they must consult several volumes of fine print.

Similarly, while OSHA has compiled more than 4,000 detailed regulations, safety in the American workplace is about the same as it was 25 years ago when the agency was created. (About 50% of all OSHA violations are for not keeping the forms correctly.)

The Interstate Highway System, the largest U.S. public works program since World War II, was authorized by a 1956 statute than ran 28 pages. By contrast, a transportation act passed by Congress in 1991 was 10 times longer.

One Congressional witness estimated that contractors routinely bid government work 10% to 30% higher than similar work in the private sector because there is at least eight times more paperwork. In fact, the federal government itself has estimated that 289 million hours are spent each year complying with its procurement procedures.

Government's slowness in the area of information value-added impedes the economy. Take the new air traffic control system which the Federal Aviation Administration is supposed to install around the country. This 17 billion dollar project is already years behind schedule. Meanwhile, the old system, based on 1960s technology, is falling apart under the strain of burgeoning air traffic.

Short of a catastrophe, which becomes more likely every day, no one seems to know how to speed up the process of installing the new system. At this rate, by the time the new technology is in place, billions over budget and years behind schedule, it may already be outdated.

The Value Equation

The value equation (Value = Quality/Price) applies to government just like any other institution. Relative to the enormous investments and public money being committed to government, customer expectations have generally not been met. Thus, value is in decline. An inability to meet the customer's quality and price expectations *always* results in a decline in value. Unless this decline is checked or reversed by improved quality or lower prices, large-scale value loss is inevitable.

Dissatisfaction with government has been underscored by improvements in the private sector. Arguably, government agencies are at a natural disadvantage when performing any commercial or service-delivery function. Lacking a true price mechanism, public institutions are slow to perceive shifts in customer requirements. Public institutions cannot count on margin erosion, lost market share, or declining stock values to issue wake-up calls. Few public enterprises have any long-range customer satisfaction and/or value sensors in place. As a result, by the time a value problem is finally recognized, a full-blown crisis is usually at hand. This is where many government agencies find themselves today.

A System in Entropy

Citizens are unhappy with big government because their experience with it tells them it works less well every day. It consumes more and more and produces less and less value. From an historical perspective, big government today looks increasingly like a system in entropy, winding down.

Systems experiencing entropy are slowly dying. To stave off the inevitable, they consume more and more resources, but all this does is slow the process of decline. Very often, these dying systems behave dysfunctionally as the end nears. As an old saying has it, "Those whom the Gods would destroy, they first make mad."

The average American knows some madness is afoot when total spending on welfare at the federal, state and local levels averages over 35 thousand dollars per recipient per year—and the problem of poverty and dependency only worsen. Where does the money go? Who *knows*? For sure, it is not going to poor people.

Or, consider the Legal Services Corporation (LSC), which receives some of the anti-poverty money. LSC was set up to help poor people with legal problems and over the years it has done a lot of good work. It has also used tax money to pursue its own bizarre agenda. For example, it has launched litigation aimed at obtaining vast new rights for welfare recipients and at making it difficult for Congress or the states to reduce benefits or restrict eligibility. LSC has even tried to have the Supreme Court establish a constitutional right to welfare. Attempts to limit benefits or seek changes in welfare recipients' behavior are almost invariably opposed by the LSC. The latest wave of welfare reformers in Congress will find out how formidable the LSC can be when it begins filing lawsuits on every possible procedural and technical pretext to limit reform.

When not fighting to preserve welfare, the LSC is busy defending prisoners' rights to more cable-TV channels and launching class action suits against corporations. The LSC has also thwarted attempts by local communities to evict drug dealers from public housing. Is this what the American people had in mind when they first funded the LSC through an act of Congress?

Speaking of Congress, the American people look at it in bewilderment. The deficit gets worse, even as taxes go up. In 1963, 3% of Americans were in the 28%-or-greater tax bracket; today it is 36% and climbing. Our 17,000-page tax code is so complex, it costs American business and households between 180 billion and 200 billion dollars a year just to comply with the paperwork. In fact, it is so complex, even the IRS does not know how to interpret every aspect of it.

Meanwhile, Congress has only completed one budget on time since 1974. Deadlines are regularly missed and spending-ceilings routinely are ruptured. There really are no rules in federal budgeting, just exceptions; they have become the rule.

The system is riddled with skewed incentives and bad faith. Take the 11 billion dollars appropriated for emergency relief to help Southern California rebuild after the 1994 earthquake. This 11 billion dollars only provided 8 billion in relief. Why? Because 3 billion in extras were inserted in the bill at the last minute. For example, ten million dollars was inserted to build a new Amtrak station in New York City. Another 2.3 million was put in to cover pay increases for Food and Drug Administration employees.

Old Programs Never Die

Old spending programs never die, they just grow—even when the reason for their being has long since passed. So we continue to subsidize wool production for uniforms even though it is no longer used to make them. Medicaid began life in 1967 at a budget of 1.2 billion; today, it is nearly a 100 billion dollar program. Medicare, begun as a 2.7-billion dollar effort, is on its way to 200 billion. Social Security was introduced in the 1930s to supplement the income of poor retirees. In 1965, its total budget was 17 billion; today, the average retiree has an income higher than the rest of the population, and the Social Security budget is approaching 250 billion.

At its worst, entropy moves beyond dysfunction and becomes pathological. Rather than moving towards reform and revitalization, the system behaves in ways which hasten its demise. Consider Congress' inexorable drive to raise taxes, spend more and borrow against the future through the deficit. Almost every sensible economist in the country knows this to be a terminal game, which sooner or later has to end. Yet, Congress can not stop itself. As the government apparatus grows, politicians pay for this growth with a combination of taxes and deficits, the latter being a tax on future generations.

162

Meanwhile, the American people looked on in astonishment as the House of Representatives proved incapable of managing its own small bank or post office. When the House books were finally audited in 1995, the audit firm could not even render an assessment because the accounts were in such disarray. It was, according to one member of the audit team, "the worst mess I've seen in my whole career." Only an institution blinded by arrogance or harboring a death wish would behave in a manner so designed to affront the sensibilities of the American voting public.

Doing Some Things Right

Like all value shifts, today's shift in the perceived value of government services is complex and multi-dimensional. While historic and economic factors are driving value out of big government, value within the public sector is also moving toward local government and locally controlled services. Some parts of government and the parapublic sector are even experiencing a value surge. This is certainly true of law enforcement, medical services provided outside the normal hospital setting, and education. Need and relevancy is strong in these areas, although in many cases governments are at a loss as to how to capture this new value. Those doing the best job of it are experimenting with privatization, competition and deregulation.

It is largely at the state and local level that authorities are finding new ways to provide services which drive up quality and push down cost. Sometimes, though, it takes a crisis as a catalyst. For example, after the 1994 earthquake toppled Los Angeles freeways, California suspended its thick book of procedural guidelines and, using federal aid, authorized financial incentives for speedy work. Instead of a four year trudge through the government maze, private contractors were able to re-build the Santa Monica Freeway in just 66 days—and to a higher standard than the old one.

Across the country, local authorities are experimenting with privatized road services, garbage collection, fire departments, transportation services, prisons and a host of other services once provided exclusively by public sector employees. In theory, state and local governments are well positioned to benefit from the present value crisis, if they can get their act together.

Does It Matter?

Does it matter whether government or its agencies provide value? Yes. With government and the quasi-public sector now consuming nearly half the GNP, it is simply too big to be ignored. Government agencies not only consume a huge chunk of the nation's wealth, they play a pivotal role as a spur or a brake on the private sector's value-added activities. For instance, if public school graduates cannot read, write or add, or if tax policies discourage needed savings and investment, it becomes more difficult for the private sector to compete successfully and provide value for society. This, in turn, raises dissatisfaction with government.

In fact, one area where local government definitely should seize the initiative is public education. Schools are clearly experiencing value decline, and we cannot afford to fail here. A worker equipped with a first-class education and appropriate job training has a significant competitive advantage over someone who is illiterate or untrained. All things being equal, better-educated, more highly skilled employees are more productive. Unfortunately, public education, the institution we most rely on for this purpose, is facing a crisis of legitimacy. A recent poll of school superintendents showed 68% believed schools were doing a good job of preparing students for the workplace, but only 4% of business executives agreed.

Shoring Up Monopolistic Prerogatives

Admittedly, broad generalizations regarding the state of public education are unfair to those pockets of excellence which do exist within the system. Having some schools which work, does not change the fact that the bulk of the system is perceived as a failure by its customers, the parents and citizens whose taxes pay the bills. These consumers, not surprisingly, have already rendered a verdict on the public system, and it is not a vote of confidence. Vouchers and other privatization schemes abound.

Parents are fleeing the "free" public education system on an unprecedented scale. Many are putting their children in parochial schools or private schools at enormous personal expense, or even educating them at home. If a private company experienced this level of share loss, the management team and board of directors would be beside themselves with panic. Educators seem not to be. On the contrary, most of the intellectual energy within the system is being devoted to shoring up its monopolistic prerogatives. Whether accurately or not, the public perceives that the teacher unions, for example, would rather fight vouchers than improve the system.

It is only a matter of time before citizens start to balk at paying for a system they are not using and which produces such poor results. Meanwhile, public education and its associated bureaucracy go blithely along, as if nothing is wrong. At best they are prepared to entertain improvements at the margin of the system.

Teachers, administrators and unions are kidding themselves if they believe the status quo is sustainable. Like it or not, public education will be pushed, pulled or dragged into a period of radical reform within a few years. Why? Because we cannot fix the U.S. economy without fixing U.S. education.

To see how closely these are tied together, just reflect on these facts from the National Alliance of Business report on marketplace trends:

- In the 1980s, 20% to 40% of those displaced from jobs were functionally illiterate.
- Over one-fifth of all dislocated workers lack a high-school education.
- By decade's end, 5 to 15 million manufacturing jobs will require different skills from today's, while an equal number of service jobs will be obsolete.

Unless public education is improved, our society will continue to split into two worlds. One will be well educated, computer literate and well paid...the other will be poorly educated, computer illiterate and poorly compensated, if they can find work at all. Those who cannot hold jobs will become dependent on government assistance or resort to crime. Over time, those who work and pay the bills will grow increasingly resentful of those who do not work. In such a scenario, conflict is inevitable.

The ancient Greeks had a saying, "What is necessary is possible," and so it is today with public education. With the right incentives and willingness to experiment, U.S. public education can be put back on a sound footing. Tinkering with the system will not be enough. What is required is wholesale reform and this cannot happen until incentives are altered. A voucher system may not be a panacea, but it is not a bad place to begin.

Redefinition, Not Reform

There is considerable talk these days about reforming or reinventing government. These debates will become louder and more shrill as government continues to experience ever greater irrelevancy. But reforming government does not mean fixing or improving the existing outdated apparatus. Something larger is required. Government must redefine its reason for being and rediscover new sources of relevancy.

It has been suggested that information technology can be used as a means of reforming government. Such suggestions completely miss the point. Information technology alone cannot reform an obsolete system. High tech interventions can no more reverse value decline in government than the Gutenberg press could have been used to save the Holy Roman Empire. What is required is a revolution of the mind, as government redefines itself in the context of growth and abundance.

Even with an ecosystem-like economy, there is a role for government. It lies less in "doing" things for people than it does in generating the conditions for wealth creation. This, very often, means less government, not more. Government's primary role has changed from one of social engineering in an age of scarcity, to creating the conditions for wealth in an age of abundance. Until government recognizes the dramatic nature of this shift in roles, it will continue to hemorrhage value and flirt with extinction.

The public sector must overhaul itself as dramatically as did the private sector, perhaps even more so. It must endure its own storm of creative destruction. In preparing itself for the coming changes, the public sector would be well advised to take a look at the private sector's experience and begin searching for value. The private sector recovery of the 1980s was rooted in a value revolution activated by dramatic changes in customer requirements...and this "new" value was derived from knowledge and information. That is as good a starting place as any for government to begin its process of renewal.

166

A little rebellion now and then is a good thing.
—Thomas Jefferson

Chapter 11

IN SEARCH OF A NEW VALUE FORMULA
FOR GOVERNMENT

Perhaps the most dramatic reflection of the value crisis in government is seen in how people think. Not so very long ago, in the 1960s and early 70s, most of us *really believed* government could solve the complex problems faced by modern society. In those days, we thought government could positively impact poverty, education or economic growth.

Today, as a result of bitter experience, fewer and fewer see government as offering any magic solutions. Many people, in fact, are even coming to view government as a source of problems rather than a solution. What this shift indicates is doubt about government's capacity to add value for society. If government is to stay in business, it must begin today to change people's minds by changing its performance.

Time is running out. Whatever the present level of cynicism regarding government, it will only increase in the coming years as government after government throughout the Western world is forced to abandon insolvent entitlement programs.

In North America, this default on a 50-year-old promise will have the same effect as a major national or corporate default. A whole generation of citizens raised on the myth of government's capacity and willingness to provide for them are in for a shock. When the reality of the "default" sinks in, it will shatter what is left of government's institutional credibility. The value hemorrhage which government institutions are already experiencing will be dramatically accelerated by the failure of middle-class welfare programs, such as Medicare and Social Security. It will shatter confidence for a generation. In our lifetime, people are not likely to ever again fully trust government with critical social and economic mandates. The blank check will be withdrawn and legal constraints will be put on government's propensity to pledge tomorrow's revenue against today's political imperatives. The proposed balanced-budget amendment is only the first and most spectacular of what will be a series of attempts to constrain government's spending capacity. These constraints are already being put into place in a number of U.S. states and Canadian provinces.

Principles and Premises

The ultimate aim of any economic strategy is growth, not pain. This should come as good news to politicians, who hate to talk about pain or sacrifice; they would prefer to focus on "happy talk" and on what they are going to do for us. The time for happy talk is over; we have let the problem of the deficit drift for so long, some pain is now inevitable, but it will not be unbearable. Mexico, under Carlos Salinas, or the United Kingdom, under Margaret Thatcher, did not implode with agony when they balanced their budgets. Nations with balanced budgets are not shabby, unhappy places. To the contrary, the opposite is usually true; those whose finances are out of control usually suffer the most.

In any case, we can not put the problem off any longer. We need more jobs, more business opportunities, and a rising standard of living—and all of this presupposes we can get our fiscal house in order.

Most successful national growth models are based on a handful of simple economic principles and premises. Consider these:

1. *In any economy, you get more of what you subsidize and less of what you tax*. Think of this as the second rule of economics, after the fundamental law of supply and demand. So if you tax investment and savings and subsidize debt, you will get more debt and less investment, it is that simple.

2. *All things being equal, the private sector is inherently more productive than the public sector*. The weight of evidence here is overwhelming. This does not negate the important roles the public sector can play within the economy, but it does provide a moderating principle for determining how much of the economy should be consumed by government.

3. *Public money is best invested in areas that provide the greatest economic leverage, not the greatest political advantage*. Investments in

education and infrastructure, for example, usually provide much higher economic returns to society than transfer payments to federal retirees.

4. *Access to large, efficient capital markets is a prerequisite to prosperity*. If there is no money, there is no growth. So it is important to encourage local savings and to make money from abroad welcome. This implies a respect for private property and a legal—preferably constitutional—constraint on the state's natural propensity to confiscate wealth.

5. *Open markets encourage efficiency through competition*. They also encourage trade, which in turn stimulates economic growth. Open markets create a virtuous cycle in which trade raises both living standards and growth and brings on yet more trade.

6. *All things being equal, the high-quality, low-cost producer will prevail in any competition*. Quality—whether in education, in products and services, or government—really does count.

Underpinning these premises are two very important and bedrock economic principles: 1) productivity is the key to prosperity, and 2) investment holds the key to productivity. If you remember nothing else about this chapter, remember these two, because they are so important. The relationship between investment and productivity is the linchpin of prosperity. Forget this relationship, and you can forget about increased productivity and economic growth.

Objectives on the Road to Restoring Value

Government, if it wishes to stay in business, must actively seek out a new value-added formula to promote long-term growth. Like any institution in trouble, it must rethink its existing strategies and be prepared to experiment with new alternatives. By way of advice, government should keep in mind the following objectives as it seeks to reverse the loss of value:

1. *Retrench*...Like any organization which has overreached itself, government should pull back to is core competencies. It must get out of activities for which it has little competence, and it should stop reinforcing failure by pursuing initiatives which are clearly not working. As it assesses which businesses it should be in, government should strive to "contract out" as many services as possible to the private sector. Why? Because history shows that government has a better chance of proving

itself competent as a regulator and developer of policy than as an implementor.

2. *Nurture Growth*...Government should stop using economic policy as a tool for social engineering. The aim of economic policy should be to nurture long-term growth. That, in turn, will generate wealth, a portion of which can be taxed and allocated to social programs. Wealth must first be created before it can be redistributed. When governments forget this sequence and mix the two, they inevitably distort the economy and slow the wealth-creation process.

On the monetary side, the central bank should focus primarily on protecting the integrity and purchasing power of the currency. The implications of living by these two principles are profound because these will not allow politicians to subordinate economic imperatives to social and political ones. Adhering to these policies creates a whole new game.

3. *Focus on the Truly Needy*...Government's social agenda should focus primarily on those who need help—the poor, and particularly children in poverty. And those programs should foster independence, not dependency. Entitlement programs for the middle class and wealthy, such as Medicare and Social Security, must be scaled back and made means-tested. We cannot go on spending 10 times as much public money on old people as we do on children. No society with such skewed priorities can produce a healthy economy and/or long term stability. Pulling off this policy shift will necessitate an honest and extended dialogue with the American people.

4. *Get Closer to the Customers*...Government services should be provided as close as possible to the constituents who use them. It is no accident the level of dissatisfaction with government increases in direct proportion to the distance from its customers. Nor is it surprising that cities and counties have generally been the most innovative in exploring new methods and alternatives for delivering services. Most of the successful examples of "contracting out" and "self-help" programs have been carried out at this level of government.

5. *Find New Models*...We must seek out new models and have the courage to experiment with new approaches. In addition, we must be prepared to confront powerful constituencies who will oppose any reform that limits their ability to obtain transfer money, no matter how beneficial for the nation or the economy.

Adopting Growth-Oriented Policies

In the new millennium, government is going to have to compete for capital in a global marketplace, just like corporations do. No longer will government bonds with low interest rates be gobbled up by capital markets in search of security. Investors learned the hard way in the early 1980s that governments can and do default on debts.

Meanwhile, today's global marketplace provides an array of investment alternatives. Investors are *consumers*, too—they are buying something, whether it is growth, security, dividends, or tax advantages. And like all consumers today, they have more options.

If today's investor wants to buy government securities, he or she can shop around the world for the right product. Treasury bills are no longer the only game in town. This means that nations or states which create unpleasant or unwelcome environments for capital will find it increasingly hard to attract money.

Creating an environment which welcomes capital and encourages capital formation applies to states and provinces as well as to nations. There was a time when states, provinces, or cities could exploit their power of place to exploit the local tax base. Today, such policies are self-defeating. You no longer need to be located in California's Silicon Valley or outside of Boston to launch a high tech company. You no longer need to have your headquarters in New York to be taken seriously in advertising or financial services.

That is why states such as California, New York, and Massachusetts continued to lose jobs and investment even during the last recovery. It is no accident that these are the highest taxed states in the union. Governments everywhere are going to have to learn to help, not hinder, capital formation and the creation of wealth—or, they are going to get less of it.

The World Economic Forum, a respected Swiss research institute which holds an exclusive annual meeting in Davos, Switzerland, each year to assess global competitiveness, recently ranked government policies and their impact on competitive outcomes. It determined, for example, that the 10 countries whose policies were most conducive to competitiveness in order of ranking were: Singapore, Hong Kong, New Zealand, Malaysia, Switzerland, the United States, Chile, Thailand, Australia and Mexico. Those at the bottom of the list, such as Spain, Turkey, Belgium, Greece and Italy are, not surprisingly, experiencing relatively high unemployment and low levels of growth.

This ranking should be alarming to industrialized countries. Of the top 10 countries compared on this basis, only five are in the OECD and none are members of the European Union. On the other hand, four of the bottom 10 are members of both the European Union and the OECD.

Turning Away the Transfer Seekers

What is the antidote to the outflow of value from governments? Principally, it is to cure government of its endless quest for growth and wean ourselves from the need for more and more government. If government's imperative to grow is part of the problem America faces, the other side of the coin is the desire of large segments of the public to feed at the public trough.

Down through history, it has generally been recognized there are two ways for people to become wealthier. One is to produce more, the other is to get your hands on more of what others produce. One is a productive activity, the other a redistributional activity. The producer gives to society, the transfer seeker takes. The latter is accomplished primarily by manipulating government regulations or laws. Transfer seekers have made a conscious decision to enhance their living standard at the expense of the nation as a whole.

There was a time when manipulating government for one's own benefit was a game for the wealthy and well connected. Today, almost everyone is becoming expert at this game—it has become the pastime of thousands of special interest groups across our country. Businesses seek tariffs against competition, and unions seek minimum wage laws and laws against hiring permanent replacements for strikers. Farmers seek subsidies. Environmentalists seek regulations on industry. Plaintiffs seek damages. Postal workers seek bans on competition. Lobby groups like the AARP (American Association of Retired Persons) fight to enhance Social Security funding regardless of the long-term consequences to the economy. Trial lawyers lobby to stop tort reform which would limit their ability to prey on corporate America with lawsuits. Farmers argue against welfare reform because it might impinge on food stamps.

Mancur Olson in his 1980 book, THE RISE AND DECLINE OF NATIONS, said a society goes into decline when special interest groups so paralyze the political and social apparatus that it is unable to adapt. In other words, a society attacked by transfer seekers can become so debilitated, it's incapable of responding to new challenges and begins to die.

Only when transfer seekers, the carriers of what author Jonathan Rauch has called "*demosclerosis*," are rooted out of the body politic, can the society regain its health. Making this same point, Olson wrote, "It follows that countries whose redistributional coalitions have been emasculated or abolished by totalitarian government or foreign occupations should grow relatively quickly after a free and stable legal order is established."

This would explain, for instance, why societies which have had their political structure destroyed, such as Germany and Japan after the Second World War, tended to grow quickly once order was restored. In such devastated societies, special interest groups which would otherwise slow the process of adaptation, are temporarily stunned or eliminated, thus allowing the society to move forward.

Special interest groups have certainly not been eliminated or even temporarily stunned in the United States. They are multiplying like rabbits...or, more precisely, like cancer cells. Over the last several decades, there has been an enormous increase in the number of special interest groups and political action committees (PACs) within the United States.

The Redistributive Game

In DEMOSCLEROSIS, Jonathan Rauch refers to the development of PACs and special interest groups as the evolution of a parasitic class within society. As Rauch points out, "In the economy, as in nature, the parasite is set apart from a mere freeloader by its ability to force its target to fend it off. You may walk away from a freeloader, but you must stop and fight a parasite."

A common characteristic of these transfer seeking groups is a disregard for the future of the country. They want the financial needs of their special interests met regardless of the long run implications for the economy. Despite the pious rhetoric surrounding their pleas, these groups do not give a hoot about justice, fairness, the economy, the country, or our children's future. They only want to go on collecting money. All this redistributive game playing costs money. More importantly, this money produces no value added for society.

Politicians have learned to play this redistributive game extremely well. They understand that simply by introducing legislation which affects an industry ("shaking the trees") they can produce a flood of interest and money from various PACs, either in favor of or opposed to the legislation.

America is not alone in playing this redistributive game. Brussels, home of the European Parliament, has 11,000 registered lobbyists and the number is growing.

Distorting the Economy

Health care offers an example of how transfer seeking distorts the economy. Health care represents 14% of GNP and is the single largest sector of the economy. Consuming almost a trillion dollars a year, U.S. health care has more economic clout than most countries. (Only Japan, Germany, and the United States have GNPs greater than a trillion dollars.)

Like the public and quasi-public sector overall, health care is experiencing a value crisis. Having been allowed to eat up one additional point of GNP every six or seven years for several decades, health care threatens to gobble up most of the economy some time in the next century. To make matters worse, much of this increase in GNP has been achieved by price increases, rather than by overall enhancements in value. Health care's share of GNP has doubled in the last 30 years, but we are not twice as healthy as we were in 1965.

In fact, as prices go up, satisfaction with the system tends to go down. By the late 80s, almost every major constituency was unhappy with the status quo. Industry complained health-care costs were undermining competitiveness. Workers were afraid to leave their jobs for fear of losing health-care benefits (which hindered America's otherwise efficient labor markets). As for patients, statistics indicate that individuals paid almost as much out of pocket money for non-conventional medical treatments, as they did for traditional health-care expenses. This shift in spending is a classic sign of value moving out.

Meanwhile, a significant sector of the U.S. population, including millions of children, remained underinsured or not insured at all. Such a situation could not go on for long in a democratic society. There was bound to be a reaction and it came in the early 1990s. The revolt manifested itself in the election of a government committed to health care reform. Beginning somewhat earlier, large corporations made it clear they were no longer willing to fund the old health care/insurance indemnity system. This opened the way for the introduction of integrated health care and capitated payments.

This revolution is only in its infancy, but is already showing signs of considerable promise. Private health care costs have been dropping for several years now and the momentum of reform is increasing. Unlike government and education, which are still largely in denial, health care is moving to reverse value declines. In fact, there is considerable reason for optimism regarding U.S. health care's capacity to reform itself. Not only are costs likely to fall, but there is a very good chance the United States— not Canada, Europe, or Japan—will emerge as the model for health-care reform in the 21st century. (For a more detailed discussion of this issue, see DON'T BLINK OR YOU'LL MISS IT: <u>The Reformation of U.S. Health Care Is Underway</u>, The Atlanta Consulting Group, 1995).

One reason American health-care costs have soared out of control in recent years, is that health care benefits have been exempt from income tax. This amounts to a huge subsidy for health care consumption. Consider this: If your company were to give you an extra thousand dollars as a cash bonus, you would have to give a large chunk of it to Uncle Sam in taxes. If the firm gave you the same amount in added health care benefits, you would pay no additional tax. Such a policy encourages people to take compensation in the form of health-care benefits instead of salary. Not surprisingly, this is precisely what is happening—as wage increases have slowed, the cost of providing health care benefits has soared. This subsidy artificially diverts resources into health care and away from other sectors of the economy, thus feeding health care inflation.

When an important service such as health care is subsidized this way, it creates a "bellows effect," which fans raging demand. This economic distortion might be worth tolerating in such cases as health care, if it resulted in better health care for society; but it does not.

The added money flowing into the industry does not necessarily improve or expand the level of service. For example, the additional funds pouring into Medicare in recent years has not necessarily helped old people. When more money is pumped into a system which has no incentives to limit consumption or improve performance, it flows through to the industry like a windfall inheritance. It enables practitioners and hospitals to raise prices, provide unnecessary services and invest in buildings and equipment they do not need. In this way, unreformed programs like Medicare mutate and drift away from their original purpose of helping the elderly. They instead become a subsidy for the industry. Attempts to alter this subsidy will bring on a chorus of appeals for "fairness, compassion and protecting the public interest." Such self-serving reactions are not new. Adam Smith commented in the 18th century, that merchants who claim that subsidies and tariffs are a patriotic duty "were by no means such fools as they who believed them."

Remember, you always get less of what you tax and more of what you subsidize. So if you subsidize health care consumption or mortgage debt, you are going to get a lot more of it.

Hard To Get Rid Of

Once in place, special transfers like subsidies or tariffs are almost impossible to remove. The honey subsidy introduced a half century ago, for heaven knows why, proves the point. No less than three Presidents have tried to remove this silly subsidy, with no success. Finally in the early 1990s, it was struck from the books after an incredible battle in Congress. Lobbies never sleep. By the time the honey subsidy was killed, the lobbyists were already back at work seeking import restrictions on low-cost honey from Asia.

In Washington, almost no subsidy or tariff is ever eliminated. Once in place, it stays there forever. Each program instantly gives birth to an organized special-interest group whose members benefit and who will do everything in their power to keep the wealth transfer mechanism in place. That is why subsidies such as those for honey, wool, and angora have remained in place for decades. There is not a rational reason to continue them. In fact, there probably was not a very good reason for starting them in the first place.

The *demosclerosis* phenomenon warns us that the threat to our democracy comes not from without, but from within.

Public Ready

As usual, the people are ahead of the politicians. The country is more ready to face up to the needed fiscal reform than their leaders are to confront them with it. For example, a recent poll showed that when asked whether they would like a tax cut or a lower deficit, most people put aside self-interest and chose a lower deficit. Even retirees, by far the largest recipients of transfer payments, stated a readiness to sacrifice some of these payments for the good of the country.

What can we learn from this? It is important not to confuse interest groups with the public interest, or the AARP with retired people, or the Veterans of Foreign Wars with veterans, or the teachers union with teachers. In the end, they are all citizens. We must push aside special interest groups and open up a mature dialogue directly with the citizens of the country. A great democracy, when given the right information, will usually make the right decision.

Available Antibiotics

Interestingly, one of the most powerful medicines for battling transfer seekers is *trade*. When a country expands trade, it automatically weakens interest groups that can thrive only within sealed borders. Winning anti-competitive favors on a world wide scale is almost impossible, at least for the present.

The best single parasite antidote in the world is the General Agreement on Tariffs and Trade (GATT), and the new World Trade Organization. By weakening lobbies, trade can help invigorate democratic government, not just the United States, but all over the world. Under GATT, dozens of countries join in weakening each others vested interests.

Other likely medicines are an *overhaul of our tax system*, a *balanced budget amendment*, and *radical reform of campaign financing*. We need to revamp our tax system to better support and sustain long-term growth. The U.S. tax code now subsidizes consumption and debt, while taxing savings and investment. This impedes economic growth because fast-growing economies need savings and investment.

The tax system subsidizes debt and consumption in a host of ways, such as deductibility for mortgage interest and health care premiums. At the same time, it punishes savings, investments, and earnings through double taxation of dividends and taxing capital gains. The income tax itself impedes growth because it discourages citizens from earning income or taking compensation in the form of income.

All this is counterproductive. Our economy needs more income and more investment, not less. Remember: you get more of what you subsidize and less of what you tax.

The balanced budget amendment would reduce the size of the pie which parasitic transfer seekers can attack. It would also put the future off limits by preventing transfer seekers from running up debts for our children to pay.

In the end, the democratic process may solve the problem by simply shrinking the amount of resources available to government. As value moves away from government and government services, people will be less and less inclined to hand over nearly half the total wealth of the nation to this badly mismanaged sector of the economy. It is a safe bet that government, at least at the federal level, will shrink in the years ahead. This may make transfer-seeking less lucrative.

As for campaign reform, the democratic process will continue to be viewed with skepticism so long as people believe elections can be bought. Congress has taken a stab at introducing election campaign reform, but only half-heartedly. The present system is so lucrative, no one on the inside really wants to upset the apple cart or should we say, the gravy train. If we are to get comprehensive campaign reform, the American people are going to have to get hopping mad and insist on it.

Finding Models that Work

Benchmarking is a Total Quality Management tool which allows organizations to compare their processes and performance with the best-in-class. By learning who does what best, we can adopt their methods and achieve similar or better results. This tool played an important role in America's quality and competitive recovery in the 1980s.

In national economic terms, this means finding and comparing ourselves to economies that are improving productivity, creating jobs, reducing income inequality, raising living standards and expanding economic growth. Once found, our task is to identify the underlying principles behind their success and then adopt or adapt them to our own situation. Inversely, if we find examples of economic failure, we should avoid mimicking them. Benchmarking may sound simple and obvious, but do not be deceived; the technique is extremely powerful.

There are plenty of people out there doing things right. The question is: are we willing to learn? We know from experience that benchmarking only works when the investigating organization is willing to *act* on what is learned from the benchmarking analysis. Up to now, it has not been national benchmarking models we lack, but the will and courage to implement the findings.

If we look at successful models of economic growth—countries which have sustained growth rates above 6 percent—we find they have a number of things in common. For one, they tend to have a smaller share of GNP controlled by the public sector. Secondly, in these fast-growing economies, public investments are concentrated in areas like education, basic health care, and infrastructure. Thirdly, marginal income tax rates also tend to be lower than in slow growth economies. Capital gains, if taxed at all, are taxed at low rates while the rate of savings tends to be high.

Would our economy grow faster if we adopted such a model? Yes. Then why haven't we done so? Because it will require significant and painful adjustments in our tax and fiscal policy and in how we think about the economy. As long as we view tax policy as a redistributive tool instead of one to promote growth, as long as we see a cut in the capital-gains tax as a giveaway to the rich instead of a strategy for wealth creation, then a high-growth economic model will never be adopted.

Our reluctance to change our wrong headed thinking and take appropriate action ought to be a source of shame as we look around the world at the sacrifices people in Eastern Europe, the Pacific Rim, or Central and South America are prepared to make in order to establish and secure their economies. Take for example, Mexico, which has balanced its budget and reduced its public debt as a percentage of GNP to 23%, compared to 50% in the United States and over 90% in Canada. To achieve this financial discipline, Mexico endured the equivalent of *five fully-implemented Gramm/Rudman budget-balancing bills.* Chile balanced its budget years ago, and Singapore constantly runs a balanced budget. Meanwhile, our government leaders seem unable to accomplish the same feat here. In short, Chile, Mexico and Singapore can do it, but the United States and Canada *cannot*! Does this sound reasonable?

179

Our resources in North America are so much greater and the sacrifices required of us are proportionally so much smaller, there is no excuse for not acting. The reason we have not acted up to now is because we have been able to sidestep the problem by borrowing against our children's future with ever increasing deficits. Global bond markets will soon close off that avenue of escape for spendthrift governments.

New Zealand: Best-in-Class Candidate

Typical business benchmarking categories are inventory management, customer service, logistics, operations and costs. For governments, the categories might include levels of growth, income inequality, pension plans, taxation levels, quality of education and fiscal reform.

The most comprehensive models of government fiscal reform have come not out of Europe or North America, but from the Pacific Rim. For example, New Zealand is emerging as a model for how a developed economy can restore fiscal discipline. Having basically gone broke in the early 80s because of irresponsible government spending, New Zealand turned over a new leaf and is now a model of fiscal discipline.

Its Fiscal Responsibility Act seeks to encourage its politicians to pursue policies in the country's long-term economic interest, rather than short-term political ones. It requires the government to maintain financial accounts similar to the private sector. These capital and operating accounts allow citizens to see how much is being spent on long-term infrastructure investments—such as roads, airports, schools, hospitals, and water-treatment plants—and how much is being spent on pork-barrel and transfer payments, which provide little long-term payback. Separating the capital and operating accounts makes it more difficult for politicians to buy votes with transfer payments because the process is more visible and accountable. To prevent politicians from, say, disguising pork barrel programs as capital expenditures, the government's books are audited yearly by an independent agency which publishes its findings.

Thus, these accounts have two benefits: they lessen the likelihood of fiscal trickery and they encourage governments to focus on the longer-term consequences of their policies. In addition, the act states that government must run a surplus until debt is reduced to prudent levels, and then the budget must stay in rough balance over the economic cycle. The

New Zealanders defined "prudent" levels as a ratio of net debt to GNP below 30% in the short term and 20% in the long term. The act requires full disclosure of information to allow for closer scrutiny of budget policy by Parliament, the press, and the public. For example, the government must publish a fully audited assessment of its finances just before an election to reduce the risk of a pre-election spending binge.

When coupled with New Zealand's Reserve Bank Act, a model of central bank independence which has greatly enhanced the credibility of the country's monetary policy, New Zealand now probably has the best framework for monetary and fiscal policy anywhere in the world. This all came about when the citizens put the tax-and-spend government apparatus under trusteeship. They then put legal constraints on government's capacity to ever again break loose and plunge the country into financial chaos. It is a harbinger of things to come.

East Asian Miracles

Other powerful and contemporary models are also found on the Pacific Rim. A recent World Bank study entitled, *"The East Asian Miracles,"* analyzed the factors contributing to the phenomenal growth of Taiwan, Korea, Hong Kong and Singapore. Interestingly, the report's conclusions dispute conventional wisdom that industrial policy and government direction of the economy were central to the success of these states.

On the contrary, it would appear that government direction, industrial policies and public subsidies played secondary roles to what the report's authors call "economic fundamentals." High savings rates, high investment rates, low taxes, fiscal discipline, convertible currencies, access to capital markets, and secure property rights are all included under this heading and were viewed as being much more important to the success of these economies than government industrial policies.

These governments also helped their economies grow by investing in sectors and activities which provided high economic leverage, such as education, health care, and infrastructure (such as roads, utilities, airports, sewage systems, and telecommunications.) It is these fundamentals, coupled with access to rich markets such as the United States, which propelled these small Asian nations from underdeveloped to developed status in one generation. The World Bank study gives considerable credit to the United States for providing these developing economies with access to markets at a critical time in their development.

Singapore, one of those East Asian "miracles," has turned itself into an "intelligent island." Investing heavily in education, it is also wired the whole city-state for high-tech communications. In fact, it is the only state in the world which is 100% wired for ISDN (Integrated Systems Digital Network) protocols, which allow simultaneous voice and data transmissions. Singapore also has invested heavily in digital-systems infrastructure such as its "Portnet," which has helped make it the most efficient container port in the world. It has set up similar systems for financial services.

Doing Things Right

Chile, as much a part of the Pacific Rim as of Latin America, has propelled itself toward developed status with astonishing speed and confidence. Inflation is now in the single digits and falling. Foreign exchange reserves are high and growing. The government consistently runs a healthy budget surplus.

By the mid-1990s, exports were growing at 25% a year, foreign investment accounted for almost 10% of gross domestic product, and unemployment was less than 6%. The population living below the poverty line had declined from more than 40% to less than 28% and continues to drop.

Meanwhile, Chile's privatized national pension plan is considered by many to be the best in the world. It has raised national savings rate and created a badly needed pool of domestic capital for investment. On every count, Chile's pension plan is a model that North America's unfunded and underfunded public pension plans would do well to emulate.

How was all this accomplished? By doing things right. For starters, taxes were lowered, the percentage of GNP controlled by the state was rolled back from 33% to 23%, and state industries were privatized. At the same time, the economy was largely de-regulated, tariffs lowered, and foreign investment welcomed.

Chile's road to prosperity has not been without bumps. In the 1980s, it experienced a run on its currency similar to what Mexico endured in 1995. But from that experience, Chilean authorities concluded they needed policies to encourage domestic savings, discourage short-term capital coming in and out of the economy, and make long-term investment welcome.

Morality and Balance

To the economic principles evident in these foreign success stories, we must add a moral one: successful economies seem to be rooted in a value system which places a premium on future prosperity. Decisions regarding present consumption are always weighed against future economic health. Applied to America, this means we have a responsibility to leave behind to our children an economy and a world at least as viable as the one we received from our parents. It is immoral to pass on intergenerational debt, environmental degradation or an education system which will not adequately prepare them for the 21st century. They will have enough to contend with in the future without us burdening them with problems we refused to face in our lifetime. To do justice to our children, we must bring the federal budget into balance and keep it there for some time, as we grow our way out of our fiscal bind.

Balancing the budget should not and need not be done on the backs of the poor. It's important that we maintain a sense of balance and fairness. History teaches that, if left unaltered and untended, the gap between rich and poor will widen indefinitely. This, in turn, leads to social disorder. One of the great lessons which historians Will and Ariel Durant drew from their monumental lifetime study of civilization is that societies which allow the gap between rich and poor to grow indefinitely face the prospect of social disintegration. Thus, it's essential that we focus attention on raising productivity and maintaining redistributive programs aimed at the truly needy.

Here is our quandary. Without some concerted effort to reduce the gap between rich and poor, it will grow indefinitely, to the point where social disorder and even collapse are likely. If taxes are raised too high or public consumption grows too quickly, it slows growth and makes social inequality even worse. Remember, the gap between rich and poor is widest in economies with slow growth and declining productivity.

Our problem, then, is one of balance. In our desire to do good things for people, we forgot that the list of good things to do is limitless, while the resources of society are not. In our desire to say "yes" to everyone and every need, we mustn't unwittingly say "no" to future prosperity

183

by undermining society's capacity to create the very wealth needed to meet those needs.

We must strive to restore balance. While not eliminating all redistributive programs, we must roll back many of them, especially those not aimed exclusively at helping the poor. The bulk of government redistributive programs today direct money not to the poor, but to the middle class and even the wealthy. To sustain our middle class welfare system, we are overtaxing the productive sectors of our economy to the point of diminishing returns, and piling up debt for our children and grandchildren to pay. Meanwhile, it can be persuasively argued, the United States does not do enough to help its poor children. As we said, a society which spends 10 times as much on old people (who vote) as it does on children (who do not) is headed for trouble. This clearly represents an unsustainable situation, but luckily, it is fixable, if we have the courage to step up to the challenge now.

The key is to acknowledge that what we're doing at present is no longer working. The vast majority of the public already knows that truth. It is just a question of Washington, or Ottawa, or Paris admitting what everyone already knows—and then having the courage to do something about it. Until they do, political partisanship will inhibit our ability to form a consensus for action.

The moment a politician of conscience, on either side, steps up to the problem of entitlements, the other side sees it as an opportunity for demagoguery. This may be good politics, but it's bad nation-building, and it's going to catch up with us sooner or later. It is this amoral, politics-as-usual behavior which had led to increased cynicism and loss of confidence in government. That erosion of respect is the real root of today's value dilemma in Washington.

However, this is not unique to our era. In the fourth century B.C., the Athenian philosopher Sophocles wrote *Antigone*, a tragedy about a ruler who, with the best of intentions, makes an unwise decision and is doomed even after to choose between two equally evil alternatives. The only way out of this dilemma is to admit the initial mistake, but the doomed leader cannot bring himself to do so. *Antigone* is an old story which tells a timeless truth. Sadly, the tragedy of *Antigone* is being played out today in capitals throughout the western world.

184

Part V

Transitioning to

Tomorrow

*This time, like all times, is a very good one, if we but
know what to do with it.*
                    —*Ralph Waldo Emerson*

Chapter 12

COMING TO GRIPS WITH THE AGE OF ABUNDANCE

Huge consumer superstores spring up in every town…and the Berlin Wall comes down. NAFTA passes…and the Internet mushrooms. The Mexican peso collapses…and the software industry explodes.

At first glance, such events may seem random and unrelated, however, they are not. Like billiard balls scattering in all directions and ricocheting noisily off one another, these seemingly purposeless happenings all have been set in motion by strong, definable forces. But in the billiards game we call the world economy, there are no pauses to chalk up the cues or study the table. And there is no point in waiting for the balls to slow down so we can reflect and learn. They *will not*.

In the global billiards game, we must learn on the go. The challenge for us, as players and observers, is to find the patterns which link these events and provide some measure of coherence. A new world order really is taking shape right before our eyes. Power is shifting from place to people, from the nation-state to the global market, and *especially* from producers to consumers. These changes are overpowering institutions, protocols, procedures, and assumptions rooted in an earlier, slower moving era.

Today's economy is as different from that which President Kennedy inherited as the Age of Napoleon was from that of Charlemagne. The most important factor in this change is *knowledge*. At one time, knowledge doubled every thousand years. Then in the 19th century, the span shrank to every 100 years. Now it's said to double every year—and the interval narrows with each passing day.

Causes and effects in the global economy are not going to slow down because knowledge isn't slowing down. In fact, one reason knowledge is growing so quickly is because it is *moving* so quickly. The minute someone introduces an important idea anywhere, it is almost instantaneously communicated around the world.

Givenchy can come up with a fashion design in Paris in the morning, and by mid-afternoon, it is being talked about in New York. And within a week, someone in China will be knocking out cheap imitations for sale to mass merchandisers. Today's ideas move quickly and can be replicated easily if the right technology is available—and if it is not, it soon will be.

Speed and Availability

An economy driven by information is characterized by two things—*speed* and *availability*. Speed is something we now take for granted. We expect packages delivered overnight, photos developed in an hour, and financial transactions performed in nanoseconds. Availability, on the other hand, is a relatively new phenomenon.

Our mindset is still shaped by an Industrial Age paradigm of scarcity, and our way of working is largely a byproduct of scarcity. Think about it. We focus energy on *managing resources, allocating materials, extracting efficiencies*, and *managing risk*. All of these are scarcity-related terms and reflect scarcity-related thinking.

These terms and this way of thinking are not about to disappear. They will lose some of their potency in the years ahead. Tomorrow's focus will shift increasingly toward abundance-related terms and concepts like *growth, adding value, creating wealth,* and *exceeding customer expectations*. In large measure, we are leaving behind the scarcity of the Industrial Age and embracing the Age of Abundance. In fact, that transition is already under way.

Knowledge vs. Abundance

There is a direct relationship between knowledge and abundance. An economy based on exploitation of resources must, of necessity, be focused on managing scarcity. After all, raw materials aren't inexhaustible.

For example, there is a lot of oil in the world. In fact, there is far more than the average person realizes. However, the supply is finite, and that fact has provided the backdrop for economic and political planning in the Industrial Age. The fortunes of countries, the design of products, the aims of diplomacy, and even the willingness to wage war has ebbed and flowed according to perceptions about the supply of oil.

Corporate policy, in general, has centered on improving the efficiency with which raw materials and other resources could be exploited. Efficient economies, such as those in North America, Japan and Europe, were able to extract ever increasing efficiency and value from these resources, thus driving up living standards.

How did they do that? By applying more and more knowledge to the exploitation process. Smart economies produced more GNP with less raw materials. That was the key to creating wealth in the Industrial Age.

An End in Itself

At some point, though, knowledge is no longer a means to an end but becomes an end in itself. When knowledge replaces raw materials as both the *source* and *object* of production, the economy has changed forever. That's where we are now.

We are no longer just applying knowledge to resources to create efficient output. Instead, we are applying knowledge to knowledge to create yet more knowledge. Knowledge has become both the critical input and output of the economy. Making knowledge productive has become an economic imperative for both business and government.

In a knowledge-driven economy, technology is the most tangible manifestation of knowledge; it is knowledge in physical form. With knowledge as the key source of value, technology can dramatically raise returns on investment and living standards. That is why developed economies in the West have sustained robust growth, sidestepping the law of diminishing returns decreed by traditional economic theory. By applying even more knowledge to the wealth-creation process, mature economies can continue to expand—*if* they encourage high rates of investment.

The Abundance Cycle

Investments in knowledge and people make technology more valuable, according to recent studies. By training people and better preparing them to use new technology, the speed of adaptation is greatly enhanced. In addition, Paul Romer and other growth theory economists have shown that the application of technology tends to increase the return on

189

investment. Thus, in a classic virtuous cycle, knowledge and technology raise the return on investment—and investment spurs more knowledge and technology. The result: abundance.

In the Industrial Age, this process of leveraging knowledge to create wealth showed us how to exploit resources more efficiently. This old cycle is still running its course. The logical outcome of this cycle is to enable us to produce energy from almost nothing—which is precisely what cold fusion will do. In fact, it is not the laws of physics but the application of sufficient knowledge that now stands between us and cold fusion. We are only one idea away from an economy in which energy will be practically free.

Meanwhile, in the Information Age economy, the power of computers and software is increasing while the cost of computing time drops. By the year 2000, computer time will be as inexpensive as using the phone. At that rate, by the early 21st century, it will be practically free. Think of what limitless, inexpensive energy, combined with limitless, expanding and inexpensive knowledge will do to the economy! The combined effect will act like an afterburner propelling the economy forward with tremendous force and speed.

Economist Paul Romer has explained how, at its core, this abundance cycle allows for a ratcheting down of the basic cost per input of production. Objects in the old industrial and agricultural economy had a near-constant price per unit. Take oranges as an example. The direct cost of producing the first 1,000 oranges is a proportion of the whole. The 999th costs about the same as the 1000th orange because each additional orange requires nearly the same amount of land, fertilizer and water as the first.

Producing ideas, on the other hand, entails a different formula. Ideas may, and often do, require a lot of investment up front. Developing software, for example, is not cheap, but once it's developed, it can be replicated quickly and often cheaply. The same applies to new product methodologies, brand concepts, or fashion ideas. This means the cost of producing future knowledge-driven wealth will decline. So, as knowledge becomes both the critical input and output of the economy, we will get richer, faster.

This means the cost of producing tomorrow's wealth is going to drop dramatically, even as the speed of production increases. This will bring on an Age of Abundance, at least for those who trade in ideas and their byproduct, technology. However, managing in an Age of Abundance will require entirely new institutional arrangements, pricing, and distribution systems. Society will also have to adjust by creating environments which actively encourage the development of knowledge and technology.

The key to business success in an Age of Abundance will be coming to grips with the two-edged sword of availability. There will be more *customers*, more *purchasing power*, more *options*, and more *opportunities*—but also more *competition*. The only way out of this conundrum will be to add more *value*.

An Age of Abundance might sound far fetched. But already there are signs of the coming abundance if you look for them. Even in these early manifestations, there are hints of what will separate winners from losers in the new economy.

IMPERATIVES IN AN AGE OF ABUNDANCE

1. Invest in Learning.

The primary means of adding value in the new economy will be information and knowledge, and the primary output will be yet more information. Just as Industrial Age organizations invested heavily to improve productivity and reliability, we now must invest in the capacity to learn. This will require a shift in thinking.

It is not hard to get an executive to buy a new machine to drive down costs. Investment in knowledge is still viewed as unorthodox. Existing Second Wave accounting practices only encourage this bias. For example, investments in equipment can be capitalized and written off over a number of years, but not so investments in knowledge. Most of these are treated as an expense which adds no residual value. As a result, new software purchases are treated as having no more residual value than pencils or paper. Investments in education and training are viewed by steely-eyed comptrollers as expenses to be minimized.

This blind spot regarding the value of information manifests itself in perverse ways. For instance, companies which spend millions on new products and services often lack reliable information on the customers they hope will buy these products. Yet, in the corporate board room, eyes glaze over at the mere mention of customer profiles and customer perception of value. In fact, most organizations know surprisingly little about the 20% of customers who provide 80% of the profits.

One is reminded of the early days of the quality movement when executives would look you in the eye and say, with a straight face, "We can't afford quality right now. It would cost too much." In short, they didn't *get* it. Today, that has all changed. Most Fortune 500 executives can explain why and how quality saves money, so as a result, quality is no longer a tough sell in the board room. Ultimately, the same will be true about investments in learning and market information.

This breakthrough in thinking will result in new strategies to operate in knowledge-intensive environments. That, in turn, will lead to the development of sophisticated listening systems to measure customer loyalty, customer perception of value, competitive cost performance, comparative process performance, and if relevant, brand equity. To know where value is going, industry must know where the customer's marginal dollar is going and why.

In an Age of Abundance, the race for success will be run on a dual track, embracing the present and the future. Companies will need to find ways to add more value to existing customer relationships. They also will need to invest in tracking value and where tomorrow's customers are heading. Playing this dual-track game will be very knowledge-intensive. Slow learners or those convinced they already know the answers will not be able to keep up.

Getting this information will be vital to business success. In short, businesses will learn fast and keep on learning. Or they just won't survive.

2. Think Global, Think Information.

Organizations which resist or get stuck in the old national, analog economy will be at risk. They will see margins evaporate, profits erode and growth possibilities disappear. In fact, any institution—commercial, political or non-profit—which stakes its future on the old Second Wave, nation-based economy will be at risk.

In an Age of Abundance, institutions built to manage in an environment of scarcity will inevitably begin to come unglued. Government, the ultimate scarcity manager—and just as often, scarcity creator—will likely find itself under particular pressure.

Scarcity, you might say, is built into the DNA code of government. Thus, it has a special knack for creating it, often with the very best of intentions. Government's capacity to create shortage—for example, through price controls, tariffs and taxation—easily rivals Mother Nature at her worst. If you want to see something become scarce, just place it under the control of a government marketing board which limits production or fixes prices below market value. If that doesn't work, try taxing it at confiscatory levels and see what happens? It will disappear. From the famines in Africa to the long gas lines in the United States during the so-called energy crisis, government—not nature—has been the prime source of scarcity.

This explains why government is having such a difficult time adjusting to the new Age of Abundance. Neither its thinking nor its tools are designed for such an environment. This, in part, explains why traditional economic tools will appear inept and ineffective in a global economy based on abundance. Both the old tools and the system for using them are beginning to wind down.

For example, efforts by government to solve unemployment with more spending—a classic Keynesian response—often backfires today because it raises the deficit and pushes up interest rates, which further slows the economy. Seeing politicians struggling with the challenges of the nascent Age of Abundance brings to mind Herbert Hoover's famous quote when asked, during the depth of the Depression, what Lincoln would have done. Hoover replied angrily, "If Lincoln were in my shoes, he would be just as perplexed as I am."

One cannot help but feel some measure of pity for national politicians and central bankers who know things are slipping out of control but who are at a loss as to what to do about it. In desperation, they keep applying the old tools, only to find they no longer work and very often make things worse.

3. Use New Measures of Success

Another herald of the new era is the breakdown of traditional measurements. Nowhere is this more evident than in the yardsticks of national wealth such as GNP, trade statistics, and productivity. In a global economy where multinational companies move ideas, designs, and products around the world with incredible ease and speed, national accounts—

tracking GNP, GDP, trade balances, and productivity—are getting harder and harder to measure.

Within free trade areas, which are essentially single economic units, does it really matter what the balance of trade is? Within NAFTA, for example, does it matter how much Canada exports or imports from the United States any more than it matters how much New York exports or imports from Vermont? Not long ago, the answer would have been an unequivocal, "Yes, it matters a lot." Today, the issue is far less clear.

That is true of productivity measures, too. Today's methods for tracking productivity are relics of the Industrial Age when things were easier to count. At best, our present productivity measures accurately reflect only what's going on in the manufacturing and agricultural sectors. But those sectors now account for less than one-third of the economy.

We are still in search of a new algorithm which reflects the true value of knowledge and technology. Part of the problem is we have no way of gauging increased quality, convenience, or safety. For instance, copiers, computers, and semiconductors have all been declining in price over the past decade, even as their power, efficiency and reliability have increased exponentially. Traditional productivity figures can not capture this tremendous increase in value.

Under today's measurement formula, a decline in price, unless accompanied by an equal decline in cost, indicates declining productivity. Would anybody today really suggest that the productivity in our semiconductor or copier industries is declining? While prices are dropping, so are costs. The real breakthroughs have come in performance and reliability which are difficult to measure.

The problem gets even more difficult when it comes to idea driven products, such as software. How do you measure the increased productivity or value of a new generation of software? Economists may not know, but the stock market does. This may explain why successful software companies enjoy such high market valuations.

Clearly, we will need new tools for measuring economic activity in a knowledge-driven economy. Precisely because these tools are so badly needed, we will almost certainly get them. One by one, you will see these new tools come on line over the next decade.

4. Expect More Competition.

A knowledge-driven economy uses fewer and fewer resources to produce more and more output. This greater availability of supply will manifest itself in more competition. As retailers or car dealers, for example, are forced to lower prices and abandon suggested retail prices, they will likely point to "intense global competition" as the cause; few will have the prescience to view the phenomenon as stemming from greater availability of output (i.e., abundance).

During these early stages of an abundance cycle, much of the economy will remain focused on managing scarcity, even as the trends point in the opposite direction. There will be some confusion and lack of certainty, as the economy lurches in one direction today, then reverses itself tomorrow.

5. Anticipate Consumer Power.

Even more than we have already seen, consumers will be in the driver's seat in the Age of Abundance. With products and services more readily available, consumers will drive quality up and drive prices down.

They will insist on more and more for less and less. They will wrest power from both corporations and the nation-state.

6. Emphasize Growth.

A rising number of new corporations, new patents, new copyrights, and a plethora of new products and services will also accompany the coming increase in supply. Suddenly "growing" your way to success would become more important than "cutting" your way there. In such an environment, governments and corporations will be increasingly obsessed with promoting innovation, creative thinking and growth.

Just as importantly, such an environment will transform the very nature of economic value. Even more than we have already seen, value will move in new directions and take on new forms. Value-added will increasingly mean information added, and knowledge will begin to displace capital, labor, and raw materials as the key to wealth creation.

7. Make way for more democracy.

The arrival of an Age of Abundance will coincide with the ascendancy of democracy on a global scale. Democracy now is on the march in Latin America, in Eastern Europe and much of Asia.

This trend represents a triumph of the individual over the state and signals a growing recognition that liberty, open markets, and the rule of law are inextricably linked to growth and prosperity. Popularly elected governments, bound by laws, subject to the oversight of the electorate, the press, and the international community are more likely to create the conditions necessary for wealth creation than are despotic or totalitarian regimes.

All other things being equal, history shows that open, democratic societies can take in and synthesize more information more quickly than closed societies. They learn faster. Thus, they create wealth more quickly. This conclusion is supported by recent studies prepared by the Institute for International Economics and by World Bank economist Surjit Bhalla. In studying 90 countries from 1973 to the early 1990s, Bhalla concluded that for all its faults, democracy seems to provide the surest foundation for prosperity and growth. This was not an ideological conclusion, but a statistical one.

Lee Kuan Yew, Singapore's leader for many years and one of the world's most successful policy makers, once said that what a country needs to develop is discipline more than democracy. But historical evidence suggests that the best possible combination for growth is, in fact, democracy *with* discipline.

8. Create New National and Global Agendas

The need to create learning societies, capable of thriving in an Age of Abundance will dramatically alter corporate, national and international agendas. As firms seek to stay ahead of shifting value and become learning organizations, society will be forced to pay more attention to the ingredients needed for wealth creation. Governments will focus less energy on using outdated Keynesian formulas for managing business cycles and focus more on managing long-term growth. This means issues like education, infrastructure, and investment will take precedent over efforts to redistribute wealth or spend our way out of each cyclical slump.

Internationally, we will begin to set a new global agenda and develop institutions capable of implementing it. Our biggest issues—international finance and banking, pollution, terrorism, nuclear proliferation, population control, war and peace—are all global in nature. No single nation-state can manage these problems alone and no existing international institutions appear up to the task. The International Monetary Fund, World Bank, OECD and even the United Nations are ill-equipped for the job ahead. They are all magnificent relics of the post-war Pax Americana. For all the good service they've provided, they are old and out of date, all hopelessly underpowered when compared to the global challenges of the 21st century. The U.N. is a prime example. Despite the good it does, the U.N. is slow, hierarchical, and too-often corrupt. It mirrors the Second Wave nation-states which gave it birth half a century ago.

However, the importance of having common rules and standards in areas such as global trade and commerce, for example, is becoming clearer each day. The rules, regulations and protocols being hammered out for regional free trade areas are the beginnings of this global process. Simultaneously, we are seeing individual groups and businesses, tired of waiting for national and international institutions to get their act together, acting for themselves to set tomorrow's rules. For instance, multinational businesses have come together to set a code of conduct to deal with child labor, pollution and community responsibility. On a global scale, we now have protocols in transportation and postal services, air transportation and air safety, and telecommunications. The Law of the Sea sets standards of behavior for shipping lines. The list grows every year.

This is just the beginning. Under the auspices of a reformed and renewed United Nations, or some other agency with an appropriate mandate, the rules governing tomorrow's global economy will take shape over the next decade. There is a Catch-22, though, to the global growth game. Order is required for growth—and growth is a prerequisite for order. We must have both. It is not sufficient to set international environmental rules, for example, if the world is too poor to care. As Gandhi pointed out, an empty stomach is a poor foundation on which to build democracy.

That point was driven home by a study by two Princeton economists on the environmental impact of NAFTA. Correlating the levels of two major pollutants with per capital income, they found that the level of pollution rises until income reaches five thousand dollars per head (in

1985 dollars adjusted for purchasing-power parity), and then starts to fall. The same pattern holds true for population growth—family size increases until income reaches about five thousand dollars per head, then falls. What this tells us is that as countries get richer, they are better able to afford to reduce pollution.

The challenge, then, for leaders in the Age of Abundance will be to slowly harmonize international standards to the highest common denominator. The worst possible outcome would be a process which forces standards downward, such as forcing the United States to lower living standards and increase pollution to compete with developing countries. Such an outcome is unsustainable environmentally and unacceptable politically, if for no other reason than it would lead to rampant isolationism and protectionism in the developed world.

The best outcome would be to steadily raise living standards and environmental protection in developing countries. And studies convincingly show that this can be achieved *only through growth*.

9. Foster Innovation and Trust

Innovation must be nurtured as the ultimate font of new wealth. That will be the ultimate competence that businesses—and society—will need in order to grow. Rules to protect patents, copyright and brands will be a prerequisite to global growth. Countries or regions which fail to protect the ideas of inventors, be it their own or their trading partners, will impede global growth and undermine their own wealth-creation capacity.

On another level, trust becomes the adhesive of growth because ideas cannot be created in a vacuum. There must be collaboration, sharing, and learning to produce ideas, and none of this can be accomplished in a world without trust.

10. Reduce the Power of Governments

Government can only retain relevancy by giving up some of its power. To come out of this a winner, government must yield some of the functions and prerogatives it has spent a half-century garnering for itself. To succeed, national governments must retrench and retreat toward those basic defense, law enforcement, and regulatory functions first envisioned in America by Jefferson, Madison and John Adams. Where services are needed, government must learn to buy them from the private sector rather than to provide them itself.

Government must develop a core competency for contracting-out delivery functions. It lacks this competency today. For example, the cost of doing business with the government is very high because the contracting process is so painfully long and expensive. Ironically, this tortuous contracting process does not improve performance. Certainly, it does not appear to have helped defense or health care suppliers. Think about it: what other customer but the government has to employ thousands of auditors and FBI investigators to police, fine, and occasionally imprison its suppliers of vital services?

Government must rethink the way it does business and have the wisdom to give power away in order to get it back. The operative word here is "*give*." If power must be wrenched from government by an angry electorate, it is unlikely to be given back any time soon.

In addition, governments everywhere must also begin paying much more attention to issues of growth. None can afford to take wealth or wealth-creation for granted any longer. In an Age of Abundance, the electorate will very quickly grow impatient with governments which do not deliver prosperity. As a wave of prosperity and growth makes itself felt in region after region around the world, the electorate in slow-growing economies will begin asking, "Why not us?" Politicians unable to provide a reasonable answer to this question will find themselves headed for early retirement.

Not Nirvana

It is important, though, to be clear about this: the coming abundance will not be uniformly distributed. While the world generally will get richer and living standards will improve, some workers and some businesses will suffer a lot. The rising tide will lift most boats but some will rise a lot faster and higher than others—and *some* will not rise at all.

Availability, the hallmark of abundance, should not be confused with perfection or paradise. For instance, the availability of high-quality jobs will not guarantee the universality of high-quality employment. Those workers lacking the necessary skills may see their earnings under pressure, and many may be unable to find employment above the minimum wage level.

Nor will business emerge unscathed. Abundance, as we mentioned, will take the form of much more opportunity but also will bring much more competition. As more and more companies enter the market, margins will come under relentless pressure. The only way to stay ahead of margin erosion will be to innovate and find ways to add value.

Thus, businesses will need to spend every hour of every day in search of ways to drive down costs, drive up quality, and increase overall value. Those not quick enough will be eliminated.

Such pressure will not only affect large, global competitors but, increasingly, local firms, too. Globalization will up the ante. Even small, local companies will find themselves forced to meet quality, cost, and service standards dictated by the world's best companies. Those unable to compete will be bought, merged, or forced to close their doors.

Thus, abundance means *"more"*—but it doesn't mean *"more of the same."* It is a safe bet that the sales volumes of some old-line firms will decline, along with margins, as buyers switch to new types of products. For example, the sales of automobiles may decline while demand for electronics, home computers, and software increases.

Governments, especially central governments, will find the Age of Abundance particularly uncomfortable. They will be under increasing pressure to keep up with fast-moving private-sector standards. In a world suspicious of slow-moving bureaucracies, government will be challenged on every front to justify its activities. This will dramatically impact public policy as government is forced to abandon or contract-out more of its functions.

On a macro economic level, governments which adopt anti-growth policies will find local constituents cranky and demanding. The global financial markets will be even harder to appease. Money will be increasingly oblivious to national borders. Finance ministers used to finding ready markets for their bonds may be shocked one day to find they can no longer sell them, even to their own citizens, who are busy investing in developing markets.

Turning Economics on Its Ear

Although the world has already begun to shift to an abundance cycle, economic theory has yet to catch up. Traditional economic theory has it that the economy's output is a function of capital and labor. Of course, we know from recent, real life experience this is mostly nonsense.

Studies now show that *knowledge* and its surrogate, *technology*, are the real catalysts for growth. Properly applied, knowledge acts as a multiplier which significantly increases the payoff from investment and raises the productivity of labor.

Knowledge and technology must be acquired in much the same way other factors of production are obtained. They must be paid for by deferring current consumption. In short, societies must actively *invest* in knowledge and technology.

Luckily, knowledge and technology are brought on by the same factors which stimulate investment—open markets, competition, and the rule of law. This means societies which limit competition or mute markets with protection, or in some way discourage profits through taxation or legislation will be in trouble. Conversely, efforts to free up and enlarge markets, enhance competition and create profit-making opportunities will spur growth faster than would be expected under traditional economic theory.

The Coming Hysteria

As we approach the end of the decade, we are closing out a century as well as a millennium. Further, we're bringing to a close an historical epoch: the post-war era of Soviet-American competition and the struggle between democracy and communism. Even now, the Cold War is hard to explain to our children, only a few years after it ended. To them, NATO is as distant a reality as the League of Nations.

With so much coming to an end at once, we can expect the lunatic fringe and even a few mainstream commentators to begin scaring the wits out of everyone with talk of a great reckoning, with dire prognostications about the end of economic life as we know it. Such shrill voices have always been with us. With the passing of the millennium, we should brace for an above-average dose of hysteria.

You will recognize this sort of scary talk when you hear it. It will be a rehash of the HOW TO SURVIVE THE COMING BAD YEARS, CLOSING CIRCLE, and ZERO-SUM SOCIETY, stuff heard at the end of the 1970s. (Naysaying seems to be a growth industry in every era. In 1963, a professor told Congress that America was becoming satiated with consumer goods like refrigerators and televisions. He predicted that as demand declined, automation would eliminate 40,000 jobs a year—and that at that rate, *every job in America would be eliminated by 1999!*)

Do not believe the new Cassandras. There will be lots of jobs and opportunities for those with the right skills. It is not that there will not be very real problems and challenges. It is important not to confuse dislocation with decay. As we leave one economic era and enter another, some disruption is inevitable. It has occurred in every major economic transition in history. Why should things be different this time around?

Thanks to the changes we are seeing today, the world is coming to where it can better manage these issues. Think about it! How could we expect to attack international pollution or nuclear proliferation when we were locked into a deadly Cold War? Our biggest concern was not attacking pollution but *being attacked* by the Soviet Union. In those days, everything took a back seat to that competition.

Positive Harbinger

One of the world's more positive harbingers of future growth is increasing trade. We are only now returning to the level of trade as a percentage of global output that characterized *la belle époque*, that era of rapidly expanding prosperity and global market integration in the late 19th and early 20th centuries. That process was derailed by a series of cataclysms—including two world wars and the Great Depression. The present trend toward rising living standards and globalization appears to be a continuation of what was interrupted three-quarters of a century ago.

Today, free of the Cold War, the world is positioning itself to deal with a new generation of problems. Those problems are "better" than the ones they are replacing. Instead of focusing on the Cold War, we can concern ourselves with pollution, nuclear proliferation, and global financial stability. We are surrounded by opportunities. The world, in its own jerky fashion, is moving toward, not away from, solutions to its problems.

What we are witnessing today is not an end, as so many are likely to predict in the next few years, but a *beginning*. The present turmoil signals the dawn of a new century, a new millennium, and a new economy. These developments are, for the most part, overwhelmingly positive. In an Age of Abundance, anything is possible. So we should stop wringing our hands about the future and get on with shaping it.

'Tomorrow Country'

The great message which emerges from a study of the migration of value and the emergence of a new economic order is that America has an unprecedented capacity to adapt and change. This should not surprise anyone, America has always been about change.

Ours is a nation of vast diversity, a cauldron of hopes, dreams and entrepreneurial energy that remakes itself every generation by taking in new people and new ideas. America is not just a country of immigrants, it is also a country of optimists— "tomorrow country," Walt Whitman called it. This bent for optimism remains as true today as when he wrote about it a century ago. So long as America maintains its optimism and sense of purpose, it can cope with almost any set of challenges.

In 1980, we faced a host of problems including the Cold War (which was heating up with the Soviet invasion of Afghanistan), the energy crisis, the Iran hostage crisis, a sick dollar, runaway inflation, astronomical interest rates, stagflation (high inflation combined with high unemployment), declining competitiveness, and low morale in the military and the country. On the whole, it was a pretty scary time. In his inaugural, President Ronald Reagan said, "Our problems will not go away overnight, but they will go away."

And although it was not a clean sweep, the problems which most vexed Americans in those days have, indeed, gone away. True, we now have a new set of problems and challenges to face. But it is also true that over the past decade, the United States successfully dealt with every one of the issues which were at the top of the national agenda in 1980. All in all, it was an impressive performance. And it was not a victory attributable to any political party or any one leader, it was a victory attributable to the American people and the amazingly flexible American economy.

America in the 1980s successfully transitioned from a Second Wave industrial and service based economy to one driven by information and knowledge. As value shifted and transformed itself, so did American business. The 80s turned out to be a period of "re-industrialization" for the United States rather than deindustrialization, as so many gloomsters predicted. We made this transition faster and more comprehensively than any other region on earth. This does not guarantee *anything* in the future, yet it remains an impressive accomplishment for a country that was supposedly down for the count.

Tomorrow's problems are no more formidable—and probably less so—than the ones we have overcome in the last 15 years. And they pale in comparison to the challenges of the past 50 years, which included winning the Second World War, rebuilding Europe and Japan, surviving the Cold War, and liberalizing world trade. America has a great track record of coming through in a crunch. In fact, the more impossible the task, the better we respond. When John Kennedy said we would go to the moon and back in the decade of the 60s, the operative technology did not exist. The plan was just another one of those crazy American dreams. Well, guess *what*!

As we look forward to the next millennium, we can confidently say the global economy is in better shape than at any time this century. Inflation is low in most of the world. Capital remains both available and affordable. We have not banished the business cycle, but we have muted it.

Asia and Latin America are booming, North America is growing briskly, and Europe and Japan are emerging from recession. Eastern Europe is getting its act together and will soon be riding a powerful growth curve. Despite a spate of ethnic conflicts in Eastern Europe, peace is trying to break out around the world—everywhere from South Africa and the Middle East to Northern Ireland. More importantly, the Cold War has ended, thereby freeing up precious resources for more productive pursuits.

There has been a dramatic expansion of regional free-trade areas in North America, South America, and Europe, as well as a strengthening of world trade through GATT and the World Trade Organization. Asia and the Middle East are beginning to set up regional free-trade areas. In fact, all around the world, free markets are in ascendance. Trade will boom in the years ahead if we can keep from stumbling into a trade war.

Politically, too, the results have turned out almost exactly as George Kennan, George Marshall, Harry Truman and the other architects of America's post-war strategy had hoped. It just took longer than they expected. Everything does.

Today, Europe and Japan are wealthy and free. The people of Eastern Europe and the former Soviet Union are able to shape their own future. Outside of Cuba, there is not a non-elected government anywhere in the Western Hemisphere. Democracy, freedom, and market economics are on the rise everywhere.

Looking ahead, we see every reason for optimism. Yes, a lot could still go wrong, but we are inclined to believe more will go right. Certainly, few generations have been afforded a scenario so rich with opportunity. Chances are, in the next century, we will see a stronger, not a weaker U.S. economy. Jobs will increase and so will productivity. National sovereignty will erode but global consumer sovereignty will fill the void.

Something will be lost but a lot more will be gained. Instead of being overwhelmed by the challenges of a new global agenda, we may find facing up to it a source of energy.

Those billiard balls are not bouncing around the table helter-skelter. There are forces driving them, and if we set our minds to it, we can harness those forces. We should be confident and aggressive about the future, not gloomy and pessimistic. We are on the edge of a new era of abundance that is rich in opportunity. The responsibility of seizing these opportunities rests with every individual, institution or corporation. Not all will have the wisdom to do so. But there will be far more winners than losers. In any case, as Shakespeare would have it, "Our fate is in our hands."

Sources:

Chapter Notes

& Bibliography

CHAPTER NOTES

Chapter 1—Through the Looking Glass

For a discussion of American competitiveness, two useful sources are: The World Economic Forum, IMED Institute, Davos, Switzerland, Report on Global Competitiveness, December, 1994; and Made In America, M. Dertouzous, R.K. Lester, R.M. Solow, MIT Press, Cambridge, MA, 1989.

For insights into the Japanese economy, those sources which are particularly useful are: More Like Us, James Fallows, Houghton Mifflin, Boston, 1989; The Buddle Economy, Christopher Wood, Atlantic Monthly Press, New York, 1992; The Enigma of Japanese Power, Karel Van Wolferen, Alfred Knopf, New York 1989; and The Sun Also Sets, Bill Emmott, Times Books–Random House, New York, 1989.

For contrasting views of the Post Cold War world, we refer the reader to: Out of Control, Zbigniew Brzezinski, Robert Stewart Books, New York,1993; and Perestroika, Harper Row Publishers, New York, 1987.

Other sources were: The Third Century, Joel Kotkin and Yoriko Kishimoto, Crown Publishers, New York 1988; An Illustrated Guide to the American Economy, Herbert Stein and Murray Foss, American Enterprise Institute, Washington, 1992; and Leadership and the New Science, Margaret J. Wheatley, Barret and Koehler, San Francisco, 1994.

Chapter 2—The New Economy: A Value-Driven Kaleidoscope

We are indebted to Canadian Economist, Nuala Beck, whose brilliant analysis of the new economy, Shifting Gears, Harper Collins Publishers, Toronto, 1993, was immensely useful in the preparation of this book. For an outstanding discussion of globalization, we refer the reader to: The Borderless World, Kenichi Ohmae, Harper Business, New York, 1990; and A Matter of Survival, Diane Francis, Key Porter Books, Toronto, 1993.

For a discussion of how global currency and financial markets are eroding national sovereignty, we refer the reader to: The Vandal's Crown, How Currency Traders Overthrew the World Central Bankers, Gregory Millman, The Free Press, New York, 1995; and Richard O'Brien's insightful work, <u>The End of Geography: Global Financial Integration</u>, The Royal Institute of International Affairs, Pinter Publishers, London, 1992.

For a thorough analysis of the East Asian's economic power, James Fallows' new book, <u>Looking at the Sun, The Rise of the New East Asian Economic and Political System</u>, Pantheon Books, New York, 1994.

For those interested in the process by which the American Military reformed itself in the 1980s, we refer the reader to Al Santoli's very readable <u>Leading the Way</u>, Random House, New York, 1993.

For a discussion of the dramatic decline in the real cost of natural resources, see Steven Moore, as quoted in <u>Market Liberalism: A Paradigm for the 21st Century</u>, edited by David Boaz and Edward H. Crane, The Kato Institute, Washington, D.C., 1993. Charles Handy's <u>Age of Paradox</u> (Harvard Business School Press, Boston, 1994), also provides useful insights into the rise of the contingent workforce and the changing shape of the modern workplace. Other sources used were:

- Price Pritchett, <u>The Employee Handbook of New Work Habits for a Radically Changing World</u> (Dallas: Pritchett & Associates, Inc., 1994)
- <u>An Illustrated Guide to the American Economy</u>, Herbert Stein and Murray Foss, American Enterprise Institute, Washington, 1992
- NBC Special Documentary, "If Japan Can...Why Can't We?," 1980. This documentary is viewed as a watershed in the US quality movement. Many view it as the emotional detonator that set off the US quality recovery.
- Congressional Committee presentation by Abraham Katz, Director of the Council for International Business, 15 Oct 94, as reported on C-Span.
- "Global Trade Expands," European Financial Times, 7 June 1994.
- "What Computers Are For," The Economist, 22 Jan 1994.
- A. Tonelson, "Beating Back Predatory Trade," Foreign Affairs, Jul-Aug, 1994.
- "The Motown Summit," McLean's Magazine, 28 Mar 1994.
- "Auto Plants Hiring Higher Skills," Wall Street Journal, 11 Mar 1994.
- "1994 INC 500 List," (13th annual ranking of the fastest growing companies, Inc. Magazine.
- "Global Economy in Change," Financial Post, May 1995, Financial Post 500 Special Edition.

- Mercosur Free Trade Area (Argentina, Brazil, Paraguay, Uruguay and soon, Chile and Bolivia) encompasses 200 million people with a combined GNP of nearly 800 billion dollars, AP, Aug 5, 1994, 18:30 EDT VO 398.
- "Secret Apple Cyberdog," USA Today, 24 Oct 94.
- "Callback Services Cut Telephone Bills to Users Abroad," Wall Street Journal, 21 June 1994.
- "Japan is Dialing 1-800-BuyAmerica," Business Week, 12 June 95.
- Dave Winter, "Bill's Bet the Company Strategy," Wired, June 1995.
- CNW Market Research, as quoted in Wall Street Journal, 3 May 1995.
- "Austrians Look to Drive a Bargain Across the Border," European Financial Times, 23 Aug 1995.
- The Gorman and Huey quotes are from Fortune, "Waking Up to the New Economy," 27 June 1994.

Chapter 3—What Causes Value to Shift?

To better understand the Xerox story, we refer the reader to Prophets in the Dark, David Kearns and David Nadler, Harper Business Books, New York, 1992. For those interested in Harley Davidson, Peter C. Reid's very readable book, Well Made in America, McGraw-Hill, New York, 1990, provides an excellent source.

For insights into the impact of information on the banking industry, read Why Banks Keep Bulking Up, Business Week, July 31, 1995. For a discussion of shifting buying patterns for automobiles, see Six Reasons People Are Buying Fewer Cars, Wall Street Journal, Wednesday, May 3, 1995, and Detroit is Retooling Its Economic Models, Wall Street Journal, August 7, 1995.

For a fascinating and insightful discussion of the interaction of technologies and ideas, read James Burke's Connections, Little, Brown & Co., Toronto, 1978.

For those interested in the impact of new materials on value, read Thomas Forester's, The Materials Revolution, MIT Press, Boston, 1988. Other sources were:
- Gerhard D. Mensch, Stalemate in Technology: Innovations Overcome the Depression, Ballinger, Cambridge, MA, 1979.

- CNW Market Research, as quoted in the Wall Street Journal, May 3, 1995
- "GM Takes Steps to Overhaul Dealership System," Wall Street Journal, 26 June 1995

Chapter 4—What's So Different About Today's Value Shifts?

For an outstanding discussion of the interaction between quality, brand power, market share and ROI, read <u>Managing Customer Value</u>, Bradley T. Gale, The Free Press, New York, 1994.

For a discussion on the birth of the cruise industry, John Maxtone-Graham's <u>Liners to the Sun</u>, Macmillan Publishing, New York, 1985; and <u>Crossing and Cruising</u>, Scribner's & Sons, New York, 1992, are excellent sources.

For definitive discussion of the role of industry-wide chains of value in creating competitive advantage, read <u>The Competitive Advantage of Nations</u>, Michael Porter, The Free Press, New York, 1990. Other useful sources were:

- "McKesson Systems, New Division of PCS Health Systems," Business Week, 23 Feb 1994.
- "The Information Wars," Fortune, 12 July 1995.
- "Laboratory in Your Lounge," Economist, 6 May 1995.

Chapter 5—Why Even Smart Firms Sometimes Act Dumb

We found Barbara Tuchman's <u>The March of Folly</u>, Cardinal Books, New York, 1990, both useful and inspirational in the preparation of this chapter. <u>Discontinuous Change</u>, by David Nadler and Robert B. Shaw, Jossey-Bass Publishers, San Francisco, 1995, was also helpful.

The Primal Change Model was the byproduct of the Atlanta Consulting Group/CPC Study, Implementation/Change Benchmarking Study conducted with IDS and American Express in November 1993. (This study pointed to <u>need</u> as being the overwhelming driver of successful change.)

Tolstoy's description of General Kutuzov's decision to originally defend and then abandon Moscow, contained in his classic work, <u>War and</u>

Peace, Leo Tolstoy, The Modern Library, Random House, New York, 1994, remains, in our view, the quintessential description of what real time executive decision making looks like. As Tolstoy shows, the process is often surrounded by chaos, pressure and inadequate information.

Margaret Wheatley's wonderful book, Leadership and the New Science, (Barret and Koehler, San Francisco, 1994), provides outstanding insights into why organizations resist learning and are so slow to change, even in the face of overwhelming need.

Laurence Miller's book, Barbarians and Bureaucrats, (Clarkson & Potter Publishers, New York, 1989), was immensely useful in analyzing the causes of organizational decay.

Those interested in the American Express story may wish to read The Credit Card Catastrophe, The 20th Century Phenomenon That Changed the World, Marty Simmons, Barricade Books, New York,1995; A Piece of the Action: How the American Middle Class Joined the Money Class, Joseph Nocera, Simon & Schuester, New York, 1994; American Express: The Unofficial History, Peter Z. Grossman, Crown Publishers, New York, 1987; and American Express Applies for a New Line of Credit, Stephen D. Solomon, New York Times Magazine, July 30, 1995.

To give context concerning the chronology of acquisitions and mergers at American Express: Between 1981 and 1987, American Express purchased a number of financial institutions which added to or expanded the company's reach into retail brokerage, investment banking, portfolio management and life insurance. American Express bought Shearson Loeb Rhodes, the fourth largest brokerage firm in the country in 1981; IDS Financial Services in 1983; Lehman Brothers in 1984 and E.F. Hutton in 1988. Shearson, Lehman and Hutton became known as Shearson Lehman Brothers. In 1987, before the acquisition of Hutton, American Express sold off 46% of Shearson Lehman Brothers. It repurchased all of the outstanding shares of Shearson Lehman in 1990 to protect the viability of the firm, its clients and its assets.

The purchase of E.F. Hutton in 1988 was the major cause of Shearson's downturn. Shearson's tangible net worth was seriously deminished by Hutton's extensive liabilities. They exascerbated the effects of the recession that cut across the securities industry, and placed an even heavier financial responsibility on American Express as Shearson's parent company.

For a discussion of the doom cycle, see <u>Discontinuous Change</u>, David Nadler (ibid). For insights into the Kodak/George Fisher story, see <u>New Chief, George Fisher, Pushes Kodak Into Digital Era</u>, Wall Street Journal, June 9, 1995, p. B1-4.

A useful source for change management is Peter F. Drucker's <u>The Five Deadly Business Sins</u>, Wall Street Journal, October 21, 1993, Editorial Page. For a thoughtful discussion of the impact of disruptive technologies on change, see <u>Disruptive Technologies: Catching the Wave</u>, Joseph L. Bower and Clayton M. Cristensen, Harvard Business Review, Jan-Feb, 1995.

Chapter 6—How You Can Track the Movement of Value in Your Industry

The market valuation chart in this chapter was provided by Ryan & Whetmore, PC, Silver Spring MD. Economic Value Added™ (EVA), as discussed in this chapter, is a proprietary product trademarked to Sterns, Stewart and Company, New York.

The work of CDI Decision, Inc., was very helpful in helping parts of this chapter dealing with value inflow and outflow, as well as value migration. The latter term, value migration, is trademarked to CDI.

Discussions of the enigma code can be found in <u>The Enigma War</u>, Joseph Garlinksi, Charles Schribner & Sons, New York, 1979; <u>Eager Against the Sun</u>, Ronald H. Spector, The Free Press, New York 1985; and <u>A Man Called Intrepid</u>, William Stevenson, Harcourt, Brace, Jovanovich, 1976.

The use of the Primal Change Model in this Chapter is the result of findings from an Atlanta Consulting Group/CPC Study, Implementation/Change Benchmarking Study conducted with IDS and American Express in November 1993.

For a discussion of GE's forcing mechanisms, see <u>Control Your Destiny or Someone Else Will</u>, Noel Tichy and Stratford Sherman, Doubleday, New York, 1993.

For an understanding of the importance of demanding customers, read <u>The Competitive Advantage of Nations</u>, Michael Porter, (cited earlier). According to Porter, one of the most important factors in developing a world-class industry is to have demanding, world-class customers.

The Four Ring Model used in this Chapter was derived from <u>Firing on All Cylinders</u>, Jim Clemmer with Barry Sheehy and Associates, Business One Irwin, New York, 1992.

The diagram, "The Payoff From Keeping Customers," was derived from Fortune Magazine, special issue, Autumn/Winter, 1993, p. 57.

Joel Rosenfeld and the Strategic Planning Institute's PIMS (Profit Impact Market Strategy) Database was immensely helpful in the course of this work. The PIMS Database is the largest and oldest of its kind and provides an outstanding platform for measuring the interaction between quality, ROI and market share.

Chapter 7—Using Old Tools to Get a Handle on New Value

Useful sources in preparing this chapter were <u>Firing on All Cylinders</u>, Jim Clemmer with Barry Sheehy and Associates, Business One Irwin, New York, 1992; <u>The Search for Quality, An Anthology of Works</u>, Executive Excellence Publishing, Provo, Utah, 1995; and <u>The Competitive Advantage of Nations</u>, Michael Porter, The Free Press, New York, 1990.

The cellular industry discovered that its best customer segments were ten times more profitable than its worst segments. Moreover, 20% of customers accounted for 60 to 80 percent of revenue in the industry. (Duncan McDougall, <u>Know Thy Customer</u>, Wall Street Journal, Aug. 7, 1995.) Other useful sources were:

- "Term Info Letter," USA Today, 29 Mar 1995.
- "Quality, The Only Source of Sustainable Competitive Advantage," Quality Progress, June 1993.
- B. Ray Helton, "The Baldie Play," Quality Progress, February 1995.
- Barry Sheehy and James D. Robinson III, "Staying the Course," published in Executive Excellence, The Atlanta Consulting Group, 1995.
- Economic Value Added is a registered trademark of Stern, Stewart & Co., New York
- "The Real Key to Creating Wealth," Fortune, 20 Sept 1993.
- NBC Special Documentary, "If Japan Can...Why Can't We?," 1980.
- Frederick F. Reichheld and W. Earl Sasser Jr., "Zero Defects," Harvard Business Review, Sept/Oct 1990.

- Heskett, Jones, Loveman, Sasser & Schlesinger, "Putting the Service Profit Chain to Work," Harvard Business Review, Mar/Apr 1994.
- Bradley T. Gale, "Quality Comes First When Hatching Power Brands," Planning Review, July/Aug 1992.
- Aldo Papone, "Brand Value vs. Commodity Appeal," speech presented to the 34th IAA World Advertising Congress, Cancun, Mexico, May 17, 1994.
- Michael Beer, Russell Eisenstat and Bert Spector, "Why Change Programs Don't Produce Change," Harvard Business Review, Nov-Dec, 1990.
- Regis McKenna, "Real-Time Marketing," Harvard Business Review, July-August, 1995.

Chapter 8—Learning Drives the Quest for Value

For the general characteristics of the learning organization, the best sources remain Peter Senge's The Fifth Discipline, Doubleday Books, New York, 1992, and Margaret Wheatley's, Leadership and the New Science, (ibid).

For insights into the difference between a "knowing" and "learning" organization, we refer the reader to The Smarter Organization, Michael E. McGill and John W. Slocum, John Wiley & Sons, New York, 1995.

For an understanding of Mikhail Gorbachev's learning dilemma, read Perestroika, Harper Row Publishers, New York, 1987, and Gale Sheehy's, The Man Who Changed the World, New York, Harper Collins, New York, 1990.

At the Highest Levels: The Inside Story of the End of the Cold War, Michael R. Beschloss and Strobe Talbott, Little Brown, Toronto, 1993.

For a discussion on the impact of competition on innovation, a useful source was Hot Rivalry Drives Good Practices, Canadian Conference Board Report as cited in Toronto's Globe and Mail, 16 Nov 93, B-26.

For a detailed discussion of the NUMMI experience, as well as insights into the recovery of the American automobile industry, see The Reckoning, David Halberstam, William Morrow, New York, 1986 and Rude Awakening, MaryAnn Keller, William Morrow & Co., New York, 1989.

Chapter 9—Something Gained...Something Lost

For invaluable insight into the changing nature of American working demographics, see <u>The New American Workplace</u>, Eileen Appelbaum and Rosemary Batt, The ILR Press, Ithica, New York, 1994 and <u>G Forces, Reinventing the World</u>, Frank Feather, Summerhill Press, Toronto, 1989 (also provides information regarding the changing nature of work).

For re-engineering, the most popular primer remains <u>Reengineering the Corporation</u>, Michael Hammer and James Champey, Harper Business, New York, 1993.

For further evidence indicating re-engineering efforts which have not been very successful can be found in the work of Steven Pressman, published in *Challenge, The Magazine of Economic Affairs*, November/December 1994. Pressman concludes that 3 out of 4 of the success stories cited in *Reengineering the Corporation*, actually do worse than their industry average. In contrast, the October 18, 1993 *Business Week* story, Betting to Win on the Baldie Winners, showed that an investment in the stocks of Baldrige-winning firms on the day each won the award turned in an 89.2% total gain compared with a 33.1% figure for the *S&P 500* stock index.

Francis Fukuyama's new book, <u>Trust, The Social Virtues and the Creation of Prosperity</u>, (The Free Press, New York, 1995) was particularly useful in its discussion of social cohesion and its impact on capitalism.

Works we found particularly helpful with regard to the moral dilemmas which business leaders in a capitalist society must face are <u>The Executive's Compass</u>, James O'Toole, Oxford University Press, New York, 1993; <u>The Lessons of History</u>, Will and Ariel Durant, Simon & Schuster, New York, 1968; <u>A Study of History</u>, Arnold Toynbee, Dell Publishing Company, New York, 1946; and Hyler Bracey's book, <u>Managing from the Heart</u>, provided useful background for discussion of the goal of leaders in a modern economy.

For those interested in understanding the impact of the Great Depression on public policy, we recommend <u>The Age of Uncertainty</u>, John Keneth Galbraith, Houghton Mifflin, Boston, 1977; <u>The Great Crash</u>, John Keneth Galbraith, Quantum Books, New York, 1979; and <u>The Day the Market Crashed</u>, Donald Rogers, Arlington House, New York, 1971.

For the power of integrity as a business strategy, we refer the reader to <u>The Caring Company</u>, The Economist, 6 June 1992. Other sources were:

- "Corporate Downsizing Amid Record Profits," Wall Street Journal, 4 May 1995.
- Barry Sheehy, "Cutting Costs Without Cutting Your Throat, White Paper, The Atlanta Consulting Group, 1995.
- "IBM Slashes Secretaries Salaries," Wall Street Journal, 19 May 1995.
- "Making Change Stick," Fortune, 17 April 1995.
- "Today's Layoffs," New York Times, 25 June 1995.
- "Scheme to Reengineer American Business Goes Off Track," Chicago Tribune, as quoted in the Savannah News Press, 23 April 1995.

Chapter 10—Why the Public Sector is Hemorrhaging Value

Statistics on disenchantment of government came from Harris Poll, as reported in Term, Wall Street Journal, February 21, 1995, Volume 4, Number 2, Page 4. For good discussions on the fundamental problems faced by government on the cusp of the 21st century can be found in Post Capitalist Society, Peter Drucker, Harper Business, New York, 1993, and Charles Handy, Age of Paradox (cited earlier).

For a profound discussion of why government's actions so often produce perverse results, read The Death of Common Sense: How Law is Suffocating America, Philip K. Howard, Random House, New York, 1994.

For an excellent discussion of the challenges facing American education, read
Educating America, James Bowsher, John Wiley & Sons, New York, 1989.

Two sources on healthcare reform which we found particularly useful were
Restructuring Health Care, David Phillip Lathrop, Jossey-Bass Publishers, San Francisco, 1993 and Revolution: The Healthcare System Takes Shape, Russell C. Coile, Whittle Direct Books, San Francisco, 1993. We also refer the reader to The Atlanta Consulting Group's white papers, Don't Blink or You'll Miss It: The Reformation of US Health Care is Underway and Managing the Cost Imperative in Health Care.

Chapter 11—In Search of a New Value Formula for Government

For an outstanding discussion of the challenges and failings of modern liberal democracy, we found <u>Democracy Against Itself</u>, Jean-Francois Revel, MacMillan Publishers, New York, 1993, most useful.

<u>The Rise and Decline of Nations</u>, Mancur Olson, Yale University Press, New Haven, 1989 and <u>Demosclerosis: The Silent Killer of Government</u>, Jonathan Rauch, Random House, New York, 1994, provided valuable insights into the pernicious impact of vested interests on the democratic process.

The World Bank Policy Research Group report, <u>The East Asian Miracles</u>, Oxford Press, New York, 1994, provided valuable insights into the Asian tiger's sources of success as did The World Economic Forum, IMED Institute, Davos, Switzerland, <u>Report on Global Competitiveness</u>, (ibid). Other useful sources were:

- "The Great Escape," The Economist, 1 April 1995.
- "Economic Miracle or Myth," The Economist, 22 Oct 1993.

Chapter 12—Coming to Grips with the Age of Abundance

In understanding the importance of democracy and the rule of law in building prosperity, sources that were particularly valuable were <u>Trust: The Social Virtues and the Creation of Prosperity</u>, Francis Fukuyama (ibid) and <u>Why Voting is Good For You</u>, (Economic Development and Democracy in the Economist, August 27, 1994.)

To contrast the ideas associated with scarcity versus abundance, we refer the reader to <u>The Wheels of Commerce, Civilization and Capitalism, 15th to 18th Century</u>, Fernand Braudel, Harper Row Publishers, New York, 1979; George Gilder's extraordinary work, <u>Wealth and Poverty</u>, Basic Books, New York, 1981. The relationship between economic growth and environental protection is discussed in Fortune, "Growth Helps the Environment," 23 March 1992.

The work of economist Paul Romer was indispensable to the development of this chapter. For those interested in reading more about the new growth theory, we refer them to: Forbes ASAP, quarterly report, <u>A Tax</u>

Companies Might Like,Fortune, November 1, 1993, as well as "Unraveling the Mystery of Growth," The Economist, January 4, 1992.

Other articles by Romer which we found useful were "New Goods, Old Theory, and the Welfare Costs of Trade Restrictions, Journal of Development Economics 43, 1993; "The Origins of Endogenous Growth," Journal of Economic Perspectives 8, Winter, 1994; "Economic Growth," The Fortune Encyclopedia of Economics, David R. Henderson (ed.), Time Warner Books, New York, 1993; "Ideas and Things," The Economist, September 11, 1993; "Beyond Classical and Keynesian Macroeconomic Policy," Policy Options, July-August 1994; and "Economic Growth and Investment in Children," Daedalus 123, Fall 1994.

Other useful sources were: The Coming Global Boom, Charles Morris, Bantam Books, New York, 1990; G Forces, Reinventing the World, Frank Feather, (cited earlier); and Powershift, Alvin Toffler, Bantam Books, New York, 1990.

ALPHABETIZED BIBLIOGRAPHY OF SOURCES

A

The Age of Diminished Expectations, US Economic Policy in the 1990s, Paul Krugman, MIT Press, Cambridge, MA, 1991.

The Age of Paradox, Charles Handy, Harvard Business School Press, Boston, 1994.

The Age of Uncertainty, John Keneth Galbraith, Houghton Mifflin, Boston, 1977.

American Express: The Unofficial History, Peter Z. Grossman, Crown Publishers, New York, 1987

At Dawn We Slept, Gordon W. Prange, McGraw-Hill Books, Toronto, 1981.

B

Bankruptcy 1995: The Coming Collapse, Harry E. Figgie, Little Brown & Co., New York, 1993.

Barbarians to Bureaucrats, Laurence Miller, Clarkson and Potter Publishers, New York, 1989.

Beyond the Hype, Robert G. Eccles and Nitin Nohria, Harvard Business School Press, Boston, MA,1992.

The Borderless World, Kenichi Ohmae, Harper Business, New York, 1990.

The Breakthrough Strategy, Robert Schaffer, Harper Business Publishing, New York, 1988.

The Buddle Economy, Christopher Wood, Atlantic Monthly Press, New York, 1992.

C

The Change Agent's Handbook, David Hutton, ASQC Quality Press, Milwaukee, WI, 1994.

The Coming Boom, Herman Kahn, Simon & Schuster, New York, 1982.

The Coming Global Boom, Charles Morris, Bantam Books, New York, 1990.

Competing for the Future, Gary Hamel and C.K. Prahalad, Harvard Business School Press, Boston, MA, 1994.

The Competitive Advantage of Nations, Michael Porter, The Free Press, New York, 1990.

Connections, James Burke, Little, Brown & Co., Toronto, 1978.

The Credit Card Catastrophe, The 20th Century Phenomenon That Changed the World, Marty Simmons, Barricade Books, New York, 1995.

Crossing and Cruising, John Maxtone-Graham, Scribner's & Sons, New York, 1992.

D

The Death of Common Sense: How Law is Suffocating America, Philip K. Howard, Random House, New York, 1994.

The Decline of Capitalism, Arthur Jones, Thomas Crowell, New York, 1976.

The Deming Management Method, Mary Walton, Pedigree Books, New York 1986.

Democracy Against Itself, Jean-Francois Revel, MacMillan Publishers, New York, 1993.

Demosclerosis: The Silent Killer of Government, Jonathan Rauch, Random House, New York, 1994.

The Day the Market Crashed, Donald Rogers, Arlington House, New York, 1971.

The Debt and the Deficit, Robert Hailbroner and Peter Bernstein, WW Norton, New York, 1989.

Deming Management at Work, Mary Walton, Putnum & Sons, New York, 1990.

Discontinuous Change, David Nadler and Robert B. Shaw, Jossey-Bass Publishers, San Francisco, 1995.

E

The Eagle Against the Sun, Ronald H. Spector, The Free Press, New York 1985.

Economics, E.K. Hunt and Howard J. Sherman, Harper & Row, New York, 1978

Educating America, James Bowsher, John Wiley & Sons, New York, 1989.

The End of Geography: Global Financial Integration, Richard O'Brien, The Royal Institute of International Affairs, Pinter Publishers, London, 1992.

The End of Order, Charles L. Mee, E.P. Dutton, New York, 1980.

The Enigma of Japanese Power, Karel Van Wolferen, Alfred Knopf, New York 1989.

Economics on Trial, Mark Skousan, Business One Irwin, Illinois, 1991.

The Executive's Compass, James O'Toole, Oxford University Press, New York, 1993.

F

The Fifth Discipline, Peter Senge, Doubleday Books, New York, 1992.

Firing on All Cylinders, Jim Clemmer with Barry Sheehy and Associates, Business One Irwin, New York, 1992.

Five Economic Challenges, Robert Heilbroner and Lester Thurow, Prentice Hall, Englewood Cliffs, NJ, 1981.

For Good and Evil, The Impact of Taxes on the Course of Civilization, Charles Adams, Madison Books, New York, 1993.

Free to Choose, Milton and Rose Friedman, Harcourt Brace Jovanich, New York 1980.

Future Perfect, Stanley M. Davis, Addison-Wesley, New York 1987.

G

G Forces, Reinventing the World, Frank Feather, Summerhill Press, Toronto, 1989.

The Great Depression of 1990, Ravi Batra, Simon & Schuster, 1987.

The Great Crash, John Keneth Galbraith, Quantum Books, New York, 1979.

H

Hot Rivalry Drives Good Practices, Toronto's Globe and Mail, 16 November 1993, B-26.

I

The "I" of the Hurricane: Creating Corporate Energy , Art McNeil, Stoddart, Toronto, 1988.

An Illustrated Guide to the American Economy, Herbert Stein and Murray Foss, American Enterprise Institute, Washington, 1992.

Innovation and Entrepreneurship, Peter Drucker, Harper & Row Publishers, New York, 1985.

J

Japan: The Coming Collapse, Bryan Reading, Weidenfeld & Nicholson, London, 1992.

Job Creation in America, David Birch, The Free Press, New York 1987

L

Leadership and the New Science, Margaret J. Wheatley, Barret and Koehler, San Francisco, 1994.

Leading the Way, Al Santoli, Random House, New York, 1993.

Le Defi American, Jean Jacques Servan-Schreiber, Editions Denofi, Paris, 1967, Hamish Hamilton, London, 1968.

The Lessons of History, Will and Ariel Durant, Simon & Schuster, New York, 1968.

A Life in Our Times, John Keneth Galbraith, Houghton Mifflin, Boston, 1981.

Liners to the Sun, John Maxtone-Graham, Macmillan Publishing, New York, 1985.

Looking at the Sun, The Rise of the New East Asian Economic and Political System, James Fallows, Pantheon Books, New York, 1994.

M

Made In America, M. Dertouzous, R.K. Lester and R.M. Solow, MIT Press, Cambridge, MA, 1989.

Made In Japan, Akio Morita, E.P. Dutton, New York, 1986.

Making it in America, Jerry Jasinowski and Robert Hamrin, Simon & Schuster, New York, 1995.

Managing Customer Value, Bradley T. Gale, The Free Press, New York, 1994.

The March of Folly, Barbara Tuchman, Cardinal Books, New York, 1990.

Market Liberalism: A Paradigm for the 21st Century, edited by David Boaz and Edward H. Crane, The Kato Institute, Washington, D.C., 1993.

The Materials Revolution, Thomas Forester, MIT Press, Boston, 1988.
A Matter of Survival, Diane Francis, Key Porter Books, Toronto, 1993.

Megatrends 2000, John Naisbitt and Patricia Aburdene, William Morrow & Co., New York 1990.

The Misunderstood Economy, Robert Eisner, Harvard Business School Press, Boston, MA, 1994.

The Money Lenders, Bankers and the World in Turmoil, Anthony Sampson, The Free Press, New York, 1991.

More Like Us, James Fallows, Houghton Mifflin, Boston 1989.

N

The New American Workplace, Eileen Appelbaum and Rosemary Batt, The ILR Press, Ithica, New York, 1994.

The Next Canadian Economy, Dian Cohen and Kristin Shannon, Eden Press, Montreal, 1984.

The Next Century, David Halberstam, William Morrow & Co., New York, 1991.

The Next 200 Years, Herman Kahn, William Morrow & Co, New York, 1976.

O

Out of Control, Zbigniew Brzezinski, Robert Stewart Books, New York, 1993.

Out of the Crisis, W. Edwards Deming, MIT Press, Cambridge, MA, 1986.

P

Paper Money, Adam Smith, Summit Books, New York, 1981.

Pathways to Performance, Jim Clemmer, Prima Publishing, Toronto, 1995.

Peddling Prosperity, Paul Krugman, WW Norton, New York, 1994.

Perestroika, Mikhail Gorbachev, Harper Row Publishers, New York, 1987.

A Piece of the Action: How the American Middle Class Joined the Money Class, Joseph Nocera, Simon & Schuester, New York, 1994.

Post Capitalist Society, Peter Drucker, Harper Business, New York, 1993.

Powershift, Alvin Toffler, Bantam Books, New York, 1990.

Prophets in the Dark, David Kearns and David Nadler, Harper Business Books, New York, 1992.

Q

Quality is Free, Philip Crosby, New American Library, New York, 1979.

Quality or Else, Lloyd Dobyns and Claire Crawford-Mason, Houghton Mifflin Books, Boston, MA, 1991.

R

Reagonomics: Supply-Side in Action, Bruce Bartlett, Arlington House, Westport CT, 1981.

The Reckoning, David Halberstam, William Morrow, New York, 1986.

Reengineering the Corporation, Michael Hammer and James Champey, Harper Business, New York, 1993.

Reinventing the Corporation, John Naisbitt, Patricia Aburdene, Warner Books, 1985.

Report on Global Competitveness, World Economic Forum, IMED Institute, Davos, Switzerland, December 1994.

Restructuring Health Care, David Phillip Lathrop, Jossey-Bass Publishers, San Francisco, 1993.

Revolution: The Healthcare System Takes Shape, Russell C. Coile, Whittle Direct Books, San Francisco, 1993.

The Rise and Decline of Nations, Mancur Olson, Yale University Press, New Haven, 1989.

The Rise and Fall of Great Powers, Paul Kennedy and Unwin Hyman, Random House, New York 1988.

The Rising Sun, John Toland, Random House, New York, 1970.

Rude Awakening, MaryAnn Keller, William Morrow and Co., New York, 1989.

S

The Search for Quality, An Anthology of Works, Executive Excellence Publishing, Provo, Utah, 1995.

The Service Edge, Ron Zemke, New American Library, New York, 1989.

Shifting Gears, Nuala Beck, Harper Collins Publishers, Toronto, 1993.

A Short History of Financial Euphoria, John Kenneth Galbraith, Whittle Books, New York, 1990.

The Silent War, Ira Magaziner and Mark Patinkin, Randon House, New York 1989.

The Smarter Organization, Michael E. McGill and John W. Slocum, John Wiley and Sons, New York, 1995.

The Sorcerer's Apprentices, Peter Foster, Collins, Toronto, 1982.

The Spirit of Enterprises, George Gilder, Simon & Schuster, New York, 1984.

A Study of History, Arnold Toynbee, Dell Publishing Company, New York, 1946.

The Sun Also Sets, Bill Emmott, Times Books–Random House, New York, 1989.

T

Taurus, The Car That Saved Ford, Aeric Taub, Dutton Books, New York, 1991.

The Third Century, Joel Kotkin and Yoriko Kishimoto, Crown Publishers, New York 1988.

The Third Wave, Alvin Toffler, Bantham Books, New York, 1981.

Total Customer Service, W.H. Davidow and Bro Uttal, Harper & Row, New York, 1989.

Trust, The Social Virtues and the Creation of Prosperity, Francis Fukuyama, The Free Press, New York, 1995.

Tyranny of the Status Quo, Milton and Rose Friedman, Harcourt, Brace, Jovanovich, New York 1984.

V

The Vandal's Crown, How Currency Traders Overthrew the World Central Bankers, Gregory Millman, The Free Press, New York, 1995.

The VIP Strategy, Art McNeil and Jim Clemmer, Key Porter Books, Toronto, 1988.

W

War and Peace, Leo Tolstoy, The Modern Library, Random House, New York, 1994.

Wealth and Poverty, George Gilder, Basic Books, New York, 1981.

Well Made in America, Peter C. Reid, McGraw-Hill, New York, 1990

What Went Right in the 1980s, Richard B. McKenzie, Pacific Research Institute for Public Policy, San Francisco, 1994.

The Wheels of Commerce, Civilization and Capitalism, 15th to 18th Century, Fernand Braudel, Harper Row Publishers, New York, 1979.

The World After Oil, Bruce Nussbaum, Simon & Schuster, New York, 1983

The World Challenge, Jean-Jacques Servan-Schreiber, Simon & Schuster, New York, 1980.

The Worldly Philosophers, Robert L. Heilbroner, Simon & Schuster, New York 1972.

Y

Yen! Japan's New Financial Empire, Daniel Burstein, Simon & Schuster, 1988

Z

Zero Sum Society, Lester Thurow, Basil Books, New York, 1980.

INDEX

—I—

—J—

—K—

—L—

—M—

Productivity Paradox, 44
Profound Knowledge, 126
Public Education, 103, 164, 165

—Q—

Quaker Oats, 93

—R—

Re-engineering, 52, 98, 106
Reichheld, Frederick F., 110
Relevancy, 151, 152, 154, 155, 163, 166, 198
Robinson, James III, 70, 71
Rust Belt Industries, 21
Ryder, 80, 81

—S—

Sara Lee, 18
Sasser, W. Earl Jr., 110
Schlesinger, Leonard, 90
S-curve, 59, 60, 61, 62
Sears, 4, 123, 136
Second Wave, 14, 15, 18, 20, 27, 80, 134, 137, 155, 191, 192, 197, 203
Shaklee, 112
Shea, Gordon, 143
Shearson Lehman, 70
Sheehy, Barry, 242
Sloan, Alfred, 92
Smith, Adam, 147
Sony, 116
Southwest Airlines, 4, 82
Stern, Stewart & Company, 92
Stock Valuation, 87
System Integration, 84

—T—

Taub, Eric, 121
Telecommunications Industry, 5, 19, 20, 38, 39, 44, 49, 54, 107, 181, 197
Third Wave, 13, 15, 20, 24, 26, 27, 155, 156
Toffler, Alvin, 13
Total Quality Management, 39, 42, 52, 83, 104, 126, 178
Tourism Industry, 19, 20, 24, 44, 48, 69
Toyota, 86, 116, 120, 126

—U—

—V—

—W—

—X—

About The Atlanta Consulting Group

The Atlanta Consulting Group (TACG) is an international management consulting firm which provides clients with strategy, training, measurement and communication services to achieve competitive advantage.

In its third decade of service, TACG uses a wide range of proprietary diagnostic and information management tools to support client growth, productivity and profit. TACG's focus on strategic business information rests on four principle areas of expertise: corporate analysis, market and competitive reconnaissance, alignment and quality counsel, and organizational culture development to build trust and teamwork.

Headquartered in Atlanta, Georgia, TACG has satellite offices in Savannah, New York, London, Toronto, Montreal and the D.C. area.

To share new thinking on key business issues, TACG principals regularly speak and publish. If you would like more information, please write or call:

The Atlanta Consulting Group
1600 Parkwood Circle, Suite 200
Atlanta, GA 30339
770/952-8000

About the Authors

Barry Sheehy's unique ability to predict major economic trends has influenced executives in a variety of industries and countries. He is a highly sought after speaker and an accomplished author.

His experience in quality and reengineering implementation comes from first-hand involvement in award-winning initiatives in both the public and private sectors. As a Canadian living in the United States, he has a unique perspective on the similarities and differences of what businesses are facing on both sides of the border. He most recently advised American Express on the global implementation of American Express Quality Leadership. Other clients include multinational corporations from Europe, Japan, North America, the Middle East and the Pacific Rim.

He is a contributing author to *Firing On All Cylinders, The Search for Quality*, and *Game Plans for Success*. Barry is also frequently featured in the media and has appeared in numerous newspapers and magazines, including *The National Productivity Review, Asian Productivity Digest, the Singapore Times,* and *Executive Excellence*.

As president of The Atlanta Consulting Group, **Hyler Bracey** works with organizations to create large-scale business transformation. He guides executive teams to help them focus on and gather the strategic intelligence necessary for moving their business forward.

Dr. Bracey's colorful background includes working on a tugboat, owning and managing an agri-business firm, racing stock cars, and more recently becoming a nationally acclaimed public speaker, and leading a highly successful international management consulting organization. He has a unique talent for communicating the power of integration—the human issues merged with measurable results. Thousands of individuals have been touched by his presentations on *Rebuilding Trust After Downsizing* and *Managing From the Heart*. Thousands more have benefited from reading the internationally published bestseller *Managing From the Heart* which he co-authored.

For more than twenty years, he has been an expert in the field of transformation, and has been quoted and published widely in the media, in-

cluding *Nation's Business, Executive Excellence, Entrepre* .
Banker, and *Hospital Progress*. He has also been featured ι
television, including the CBS Evening News *Eye on America* series.

Rick Frazier is a consultant with entrepreneurial roots and a strong background in the high-tech industry.

He served in various sales and marketing positions for one of the first companies to manufacture word processing equipment, one of the first companies to manufacture mini-computers, and one of the largest UNIX database software companies in the country. He also co-founded an on-line services company where he served as CEO for five years. The story of his unique start-up company and its subsequent acquisition by a Fortune 100 firm was featured in national media, including *USA Today* and *Business Week*.

Today Rick specializes in coaching executives on having the right information, at the right time to achieve ongoing competitive advantage for their organizations. He is an accomplished speaker on the issues of value, brand equity, and strategic planning.

of as part of something larger.
· "ownership."

BA

SwA
· no frills
· yet ranked highest. why?
· bec always ~~fulfill~~ expectations.
· ·· ·· difference in svc. why?
      · culture of svc.
            · paychecks "from our customer."
            · an identification w/ customer!
              empathy.
            · "we're all in this together."
      where does this commitment come from —
      ~~an~~ everyday culture
            · margins ~~tried~~ to put out of biz.
            · continual reminder
      other aspects to which we shall refer